S0-DZP-958

The MAILBOX®

grade **K**

The Busy Teacher's
SEASONAL BOOK

Our favorite holiday and seasonal activities
from the 2006–2011 issues of *The Mailbox®* magazine

- ● More than 170 activities, tips, practice pages, and patterns

- ● Features ideas for literacy, math, science, and social studies

- ● Reinforces key kindergarten skills

- ● Includes Common Core standards

- ● Fun for students and teachers!

Managing Editor: Tina Petersen

Editorial Team: Becky S. Andrews, Diane Badden, Kimberley Bruck, Karen A. Brudnak, Catherine Caudill, Pam Crane, Chris Curry, David Drews, Karen Brewer Grossman, Tazmen Fisher Hansen, Marsha Heim, Lori Z. Henry, Mark Rainey, Greg D. Rieves, Rebecca Saunders, Donna K. Teal, Sharon M. Tresino, Zane Williard

www.TheMailbox.com

©2014 The Mailbox® Books
All rights reserved.
ISBN 978-1-61276-445-0

Printed in the United States
10 9 8 7 6 5 4 3 2 1

TABLE OF CONTENTS

SEASONAL BOOKS AND TOPICS

Miss Bindergarten Gets Ready for Kindergarten 3
Favorite Back-to-School Ideas 5
Fabulous Fire Safety! 8
Nutty About Numbers 12
Bats 15
Colonial Kids 19
Wrapped Up for the Holidays 22
Frosty Fun 25
Tacky the Penguin 28
Let's Celebrate the 100th Day 30
Just for Valentine's Day! 33
Hooray for Dr. Seuss! 34
End of the Rainbow 38
Showers and Flowers 41
Bugs 46
"Toad-ally" Cool Year-End Ideas 49

MONTH BY MONTH

August 54
September 61
October 68
November 76
December 84
January 93
February 99
March 105
April 112
May 118
Summer 125

Miss Bindergarten Gets Ready for Kindergarten

Written by Joseph Slate
Illustrated by Ashley Wolff

Miss Bindergarten's students have a lot to do to get ready for kindergarten. As they wake up, brush their teeth, and find their sneakers, Miss Bindergarten completes several chores of her own! This simple, engaging book soothes kindergarten jitters and helps youngsters develop rhyming skills.

ideas by Ada Goren, Winston-Salem, NC

Getting Ready

Writing (W.K.8)

To prepare for this adorable class book, have someone take several photos of you getting ready for kindergarten. Then take a photo of each student. Arrange each two-page spread of your class book as shown, with student photos to the left and a photo of yourself to the right. As each child describes something he does to get ready for kindergarten, write his words next to his photo. Then caption each photo of yourself as shown and bind the pages together. After you read the book aloud, place it in your reading center.

Emily eats her oatmeal.

Jack goes to bed early.

Ms. Taylor gets ready for kindergarten.

Student Name Game

Matching letters (RF.K.1d)

From Adam the alligator to Zach the zebra, Miss Bindergarten's students cover the entire alphabet! That makes the class photos on the final page of the book perfect for this letter-matching game. Place a set of small uppercase letter cards at a center along with the book opened to the final page. Two students take turns choosing cards, identifying the letters, and placing them over the matching pictures.

Find the Rhyme

Identifying rhyming words (RF.K.2a)

Cut out a copy of the cards on page 4 and place them in your pocket chart. During a second reading of the story, pause before each rhyme that has a corresponding card. Encourage a student to find the card to complete the rhyme. Have youngsters help you recite the sentence with the rhyme included. Then have the student turn over the card. "Jessie Sike pedals her...bike!"

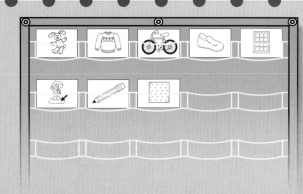

Picture Cards

Use with "Find the Rhyme" on page 3.

TEC61439

TEC61439

TEC61439

TEC61439

TEC61439

TEC61439

TEC61439

TEC61439

Favorite Back-to-School Ideas

Use these top-notch ideas from our readers to make the first days of school a success!

This is my dog Daisy.

Meeting the Teacher
Book (RI.K.10)

Once students get to know you, they're sure to feel more comfortable in your classroom. For a fun introduction, gather several photos that are likely to interest your students, such as photos of yourself at their age and photos of your pets or family. Mount the photos on sheets of paper and add simple captions. Then slide the papers into plastic page protectors and secure them in a three-ring binder. Title the resulting book "[Your name]'s Story." Read the book to students on the first day of school and then place it in your classroom library for youngsters to revisit on their own. Don't be surprised if it's one of your students' favorite reading selections!

Angela Kozeal, Tri-Center Elementary, Neola, IA

A Wonderful Place
School tour

Looking for a creative way to familiarize your students with the school? Begin with this version of "Going on a Bear Hunt." Establish a steady clapping rhythm. Then say the chant, having students echo each line and incorporate motions as appropriate. Add verses as desired.

Later, when students are not in the classroom, remove from your alphabet wall display the initial letter of each location in the chant. (As an alternative, display lettered index cards in alphabetical order and remove the appropriate cards from the sequence.) For example, remove the *o* for *office* and the *m* for *music room.* Place each letter in the actual corresponding school location. When the children return, notice with mock surprise that the letters are missing. Then take students and a camera on a letter search throughout the school. Each time you find a letter, take a photo of the letter and staff at that location. Use the photos as props during later repetitions of the chant.

We're at [Edmondson Elementary].
We're going to have fun.
What a wonderful place!
We're so glad!

I see the [office].
What do we do there?
We [call home].
[Ring, ring, ring.]

I see the [music room.]
What do we do there?
We [sing songs].
[La, la, la!]

Laura Pullen, Edmondson Elementary, Brentwood, TN

A New Crop of Students

Watermelon Welcome
Display

This bulletin board is just "ripe" for the beginning of the school year, and with a few changes you can use it throughout the fall! Have each student draw several watermelon seeds on a red construction paper semicircle. Then instruct her to glue the paper to a slightly larger white semicircle to make a watermelon slice. Post each youngster's watermelon with a personalized leaf on a board titled as shown. Arrange green paper spirals as desired to make vines.

To modify the display for later in the year, remove the watermelons but keep the leaves and vines on the board. Have each youngster paint a picture of a pumpkin or use liquid starch to adhere orange tissue paper squares all over a pumpkin cutout. Showcase each pumpkin near the corresponding youngster's leaf. Title the display "Meet Us in the Pumpkin Patch!" and add a decorative scarecrow if desired.

Casey Cooksey, Bruce Elementary, Bruce, MS

In the Spotlight
Literacy (RF.K.2b, SL.K.1)

Add pizzazz to the traditional student-of-the-day activity! Invite the honored youngster to stand with you in front of the class. Have him hold up a large card labeled with his name. Then lead students in a call-and-response cheer to spell the name. Next, have students clap once for each syllable as you say the name, and help them determine how many parts (syllables) the name has. Afterward, invite the honored youngster to tell a little about himself, such as his favorite color, food, and animal. Write the information on a sheet of paper and have him illustrate it. Showcase the resulting poster in a designated classroom area, or begin a class book of posters. Repeat the activity to give each youngster a turn in the spotlight.

Cynthia Jamnik
Our Lady Queen of Peace School
Milwaukee, WI

Namely, Writing
Literacy (RF.K.3a)

Classmates' names make this center irresistible to young learners. To introduce the activity, each week show students a letter card or manipulative for a letter that begins the first name of one or more students. Ask students to name the corresponding classmate(s). Write each identified name on a separate sentence strip and mount a photo of the corresponding person beside the name. Display the strip(s) and letter at a center stocked with writing supplies. When a student visits the center, have him practice writing the name or use it in a sentence. No doubt youngsters will be eager to find out whose name will be featured next!

Tammy Lutz, George E. Greene Elementary, Bad Axe, MI

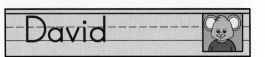

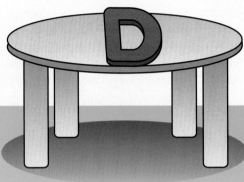

(sung to the tune of "Skip to My Lou")

[Jess] likes [soccer]. How about you?
[Jess] likes [soccer]. How about you?
[Jess] likes [soccer]. How about you?
Raise your hand if you do too.

Who Likes It?
Song

Count on this get-acquainted activity to be a hit! Sit with students in a circle. To begin, ask one student to name something that she likes to do. Then lead students in the song shown, inserting the youngster's name and activity. Repeat the song to feature each student. As youngsters learn about one another, they're bound to find out that they have a lot in common!

Suzanne Moore, Irving, TX

Just Alike!
Literacy (L.K.1f)

Build your classroom community with this class book idea. Take an individual photo of each student. Program a page like the one shown and then make one copy for every two students. Mount two photos on each copy. To complete each page, ask the two pictured youngsters to write their names below their photos. Help them determine an appropriate sentence ending, and write it on the blank. Bind the completed pages into a book titled "We Are Alike." It's a perfect read-aloud and discussion starter!

Angie Kutzer
Garrett Elementary
Mebane, NC

Fabulous Fire Safety!

These red-hot ideas are engaging and educational—and just what you need for reinforcing fire safety!

Call 9-1-1

Prepare youngsters to take action in the event of a fire! Give each child a copy of the pattern on page 9. Instruct students to press the numerals 9-1-1 on their keypads each time they sing the numbers.

(sung to the tune of "Three Blind Mice")

Nine, one, one; nine, one, one.
Call for help, call for help.
If there's a scary emergency,
There is a number, you will agree,
That will bring help for both you and me.
Nine, one, one; nine, one, one.

Christena Nelson, Copper Canyon Elementary
West Jordan, UT

Stop, Drop, and Roll!

Set aside time for each child to practice a proven fire-safety technique! Cut several flame shapes from orange and red felt. Press the felt cutouts to the clothing of a volunteer. Then, in a carpeted area, ask the child to *stop*, to *drop*, and to *roll* until the flames are no longer on his clothing. (The felt flames will stick to the carpet.) Invite each child to take a turn; then store the cutouts in a carpeted area for additional practice.

Tammy Lutz, George E. Greene Elementary, Bad Axe, MI

What's Hot?

When this sorting activity is finished, each student will have a picture-perfect reference of potential fire hazards. Give each child a copy of page 10. After naming all the pictures, have her prepare a sorting mat like the one shown. Then have her cut out the picture cards, sort them in the correct categories, and glue them in place. *(L.K.5a)*

Cheryl Mesch, Northwood Elementary, West Seneca, NY

Thank You, Firefighters!

Make this adorable poster to thank firefighters for all they do, which may include a school visit or a fire station tour. Enlarge a copy of the dog pattern on page 11 and cut it out. Provide washable black ink so students can add thumbprint spots to the canine. Glue the completed project on sturdy paper. Add a note of thanks; then invite each child to write his name on the thank-you poster.

Annette Warren, First Baptist Child Development Center, Taylorsville, NC

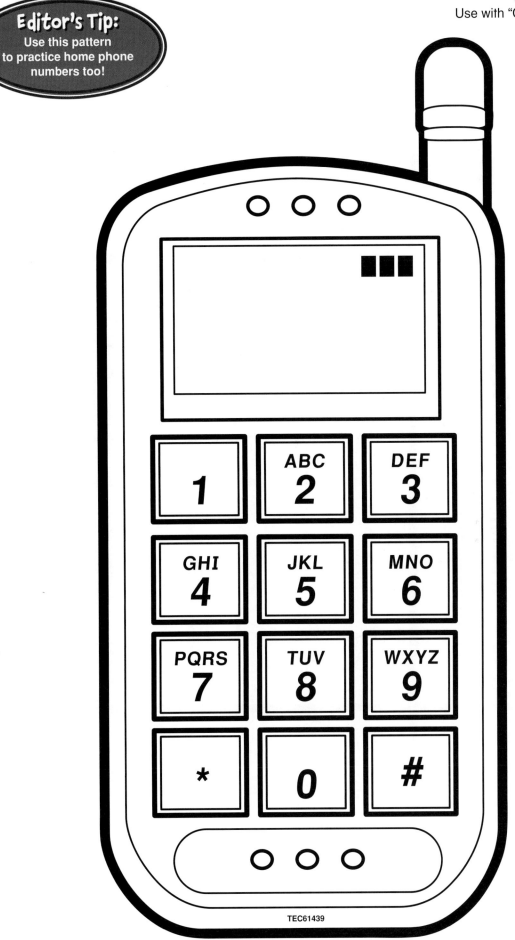

Editor's Tip:
Use this pattern to practice home phone numbers too!

TEC61439

Picture Cards

Use with "What's Hot?" on page 8.

TEC61439

TEC61439

TEC61439

TEC61439

TEC61439

TEC61439

TEC61439

TEC61439

TEC61439

TEC61439

TEC61439

TEC61439

TEC61439

Nutty About Numbers

Incorporate the fall season with this collection of number-sense ideas that are just right for your kindergartners!

ideas contributed by Gerri Primak, Charlotte, NC

Treetop Treats
Subtraction (K.OA.A.1)

For this group-time activity, cut out a copy of the acorn cards on page 14. Draw the outline of a large tree on the board. Place the acorn cards and Sticky-Tac adhesive nearby. To begin, attach some acorns to the tree and invite youngsters to count them. Then lead students in reciting the rhyme shown, inserting the number of acorns where indicated. While saying the third line of the rhyme, pretend to be a squirrel and remove some acorns from the tree. Then guide youngsters in counting the remaining acorns. To play again, place a different number of acorns on the tree.

[*Number*] little acorns
In a tree.
Along comes a squirrel—
Now how many do you see?

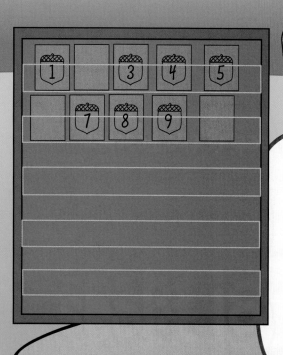

Squirrel Says
Writing numbers (K.CC.A.3)

Youngsters follow Squirrel's directions in this small-group game. To prepare, number a copy of the acorn cards on page 14 from 1 to 10 and place them in order in a pocket chart. To begin, give each student a whiteboard and marker. Then say a command such as "Squirrel says, 'Write the number five.'" Using the acorns as a reference, have each child write the announced number on his board. After checking students' work, turn over the matching number card and have youngsters wipe off their boards. Then continue for each remaining number.

Collecting Nuts

Ordering numbers through ten

To prepare this center, cut out a copy of the acorn cards on page 14 and number them from 1 to 10. Also glue a copy of a squirrel card on page 14 to a craft stick. Place the resulting squirrel puppet at a center along with the acorn cards. A child puts the acorns in order and then "walks" the squirrel by each acorn while practicing counting.

One, two, ...

So Many Squirrels

Matching numbers to sets (K.CC.B.5)

Youngsters are sure to go nutty for this version of lotto! To prepare, stack ten squirrel cards (cards on page 14) facedown in a pocket chart. Give each child ten game markers and an uncut copy of the acorn cards on page 14 to use as a lotto board. Instruct each youngster to write a different number from 1 to 10 in each acorn. To play, flip a desired number of squirrel cards. Lead the group in counting the squirrels. Then have each child cover the matching space on his board. When a child has five spaces covered in a row, he announces "Nutty numbers!" Continue until each number has been covered.

Acorns Aplenty

Comparing sets (K.CC.C.6)

Place at a center a set of number cards from 1 to 10, a brown washable ink pad, paper strips, and brown markers. A child takes two cards and copies the numbers on a paper strip as shown. Next, she makes a corresponding number of fingerprints next to each number and uses a marker to add acorn details to each print. Then she circles the set of acorns with more.

Acorn Cards

Use with "Treetop Treats" and "Squirrel Says" on page 12 and "Collecting Nuts" and "So Many Squirrels" on page 13.

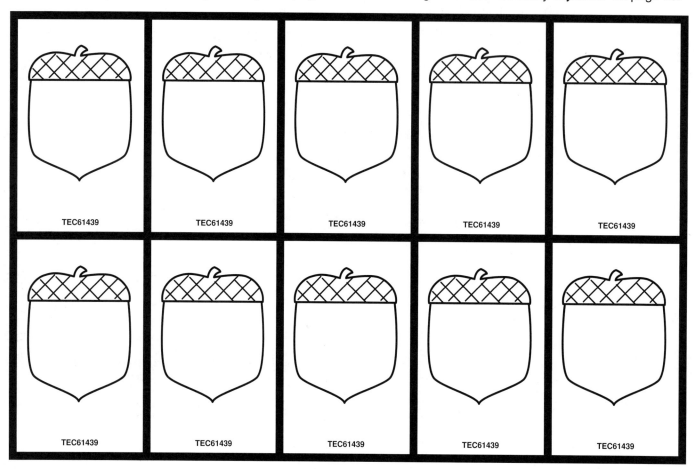

Squirrel Cards

Use with "Collecting Nuts" and "So Many Squirrels" on page 13.

Seasonal Skill Practice
Bats

MATH AND SCIENCE
Yes or No?

Activate students' prior knowledge and reveal bat facts with this simple graphing activity. Write on the board a bat-related question and draw a two-column cave-shaped chart labeled as shown. Give each child a bat cutout (pattern on page 17). Read the question aloud. Have each child indicate her response by placing a bat in the corresponding column. Then use the provided information to guide a class discussion about students' answers. Encourage students to discuss the results of the graph and then reveal the correct answer. Remove the bats and continue with more bat-related questions. *Activating prior knowledge, graphing*

adapted from an idea by Christine Kellerman
Grandma's House, Brookfield, WI

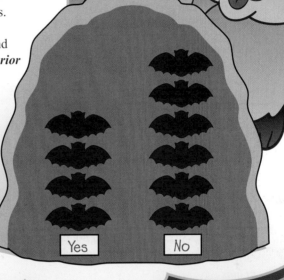

Do bats sleep at night?

Bat Facts
Bats sleep during the day and fly around at night.
Bats eat fruit or insects.
Bats have fur.
Bats sleep in caves.
Bats hang upside down.
Bats have very good hearing.

LITERACY
Wing by Wing

For this center, trace a copy of the bat pattern on page 17 onto black tagboard. Then cut out the tracing and draw a face. Place the bat at a center along with a cutout copy of the rhyming cards on page 17. A student chooses a picture and places the card on a wing. Then she finds the rhyming picture and places it on the other wing. After quietly saying the rhyming words, she removes the cards and continues with other rhyming pairs. **For an added challenge,** have the student write each rhyming pair on a sheet of paper. *Rhyming (RF.K.2a)*

adapted from an idea by Jennie Jensen
Clarence, IA

MATH
Bats in Their Places

Give each child a copy of page 18. Have him cut out the bat cards at the bottom of the page. Then read aloud the directions below to direct students where to glue their bats. After they complete the page, encourage pairs of students to use positional words to tell each other about the location of the bats. *Positional words, following directions (K.G.A.1)*

Ada Goren, Winston-Salem, NC

Directions:
1. Put a bat *above* the small tree.
2. Put a bat *below* the stars.
3. Put a bat *next to* the owl.
4. Put a bat *between* the trees.
5. Put a bat *on* the fence.
6. Put a bat *to the right* of the large tree's hole.

SCIENCE
Batty Facts

With this action poem, your youngsters will learn several facts about bats. For a literacy connection, give each child a copy of the poem. Have students circle "bat" or "bats" each time it appears in the poem. ***Characteristics of bats***

Ada Goren

Bats fly around at night
And sleep throughout the day.
If a bat flies too close to you,
You may want to run away!

Flap arms.
Rest head on folded hands.

Run in place.

Bats are helpful creatures.
They eat bugs, you know.
But do not call a bat a bird.
It has no feathers—no!

Put up index finger.
Make eating motion with hand.
Wag finger back and forth.

Bats have furry bodies
And hang down by their feet.
Now, tell me, don't you think
That bats are kind of neat?

Flap arms.
Point to feet.
Shrug shoulders.

LITERACY
Batty About Words

Use the bat pattern on page 17 to make several templates. Also display a large bat cave shape cut from bulletin board paper. Have each child trace a bat template, cut out the shape, and add facial features. Then choose an idea below.

Initial consonant *b* (RF.K.3a): Have students name words that begin with *b* like *bat*. Record students' responses on the board. After rereading the list aloud, direct each child to draw on a two-inch white paper square a word that begins with *b*. Help her add a label and glue the square to her bat. Display the bats on the cave with the title "Batty About *B*s."

Word family *-at* (RF.K.3): Assign each student an onset that makes a word when combined with *-at*. Have her blend her onset with *-at* and use a white crayon to write the resulting word on her bat. Display the bats on the cave with the title "The *-at* Cave."

Kathryn Davenport, Partin Elementary, Oviedo, FL

Bat Pattern

Use with "Yes or No?" and "Wing by Wing" on page 15 and "Batty About Words" on page 16.

Rhyming Cards

Use with "Wing by Wing" on page 15.

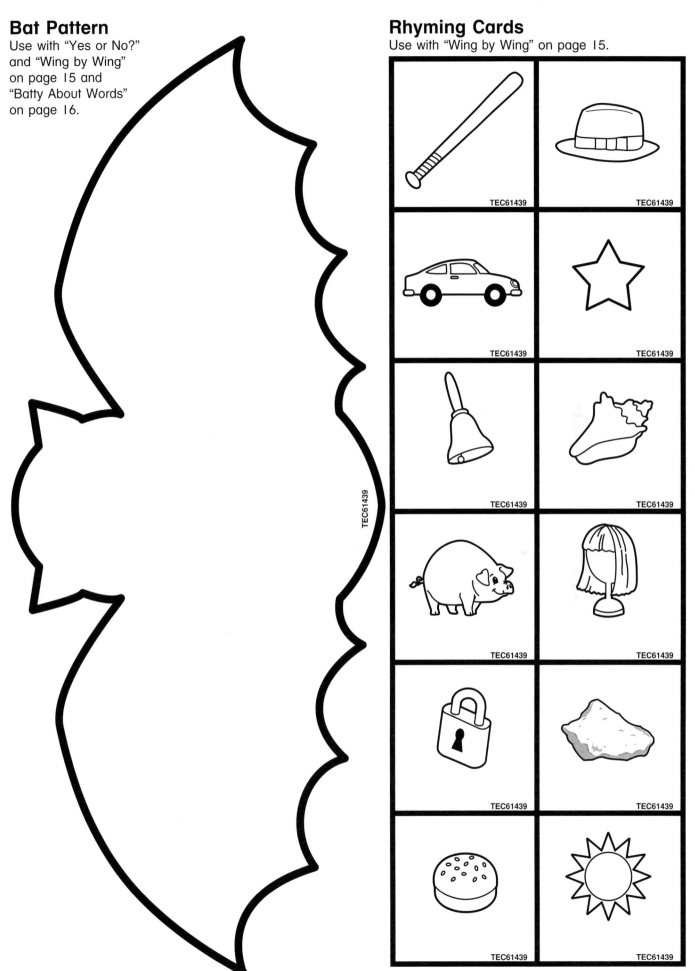

TEC61439

Name _____

18

The Busy Teacher's Seasonal Book • ©The Mailbox® Books • TEC61439

Note to the teacher: Use with "Bats in Their Places" on page 16.

Colonial Kids

ideas contributed by Laurie K. Gibbons
Huntsville, AL

Different and Alike
Identifying similarities and differences

As you teach students this song, guide them to compare their lives with the lives of colonial children.

(sung to the first verse of "My Bonnie Lies Over the Ocean")

Colonial children were different
From the children today, we know.
They worked hard from sunup to sundown
And rarely to school could they go.

Colonial children did chores then
To help with their families' needs.
They cooked and they gardened and hunted
And did different household deeds.

Colonial children were also
Like so many children today.
They laughed and learned and they had great fun
With the games they liked to play!

Colonial Cabin

Feed the chickens.

Churn some butter.

Fly a kite.

Spin a top.

Peek at the Past
Developing vocabulary

This cabin project holds reminders of how colonial children spent their time! Have each child place a copy of the cabin pattern from page 20 on a piece of corrugated paper and then do a crayon rubbing on it. After he adds any other desired crayon details, staple the top of the house to a blank sheet of paper. Then have the youngster cut out the house through both thicknesses. Next, ask the youngster to open the resulting booklet and glue an envelope facedown on the back cover, keeping the flap free. Then instruct him to color and cut out a copy of the picture cards from page 21 and store them in the envelope. Follow up with the ideas below.

Action words (L.K.1b): Read the cards' captions with students. Then have students underline the action words and act them out.

Categorizing (L.K.5a): Help students sort the cards by the categories of work, play, and school. *(Work: sampler, butter churn, and chickens; Play: hoop, top, and kite; School: hornbook and feather quill)*

Cabin Pattern
Use with "Peek at the Past" on page 19.

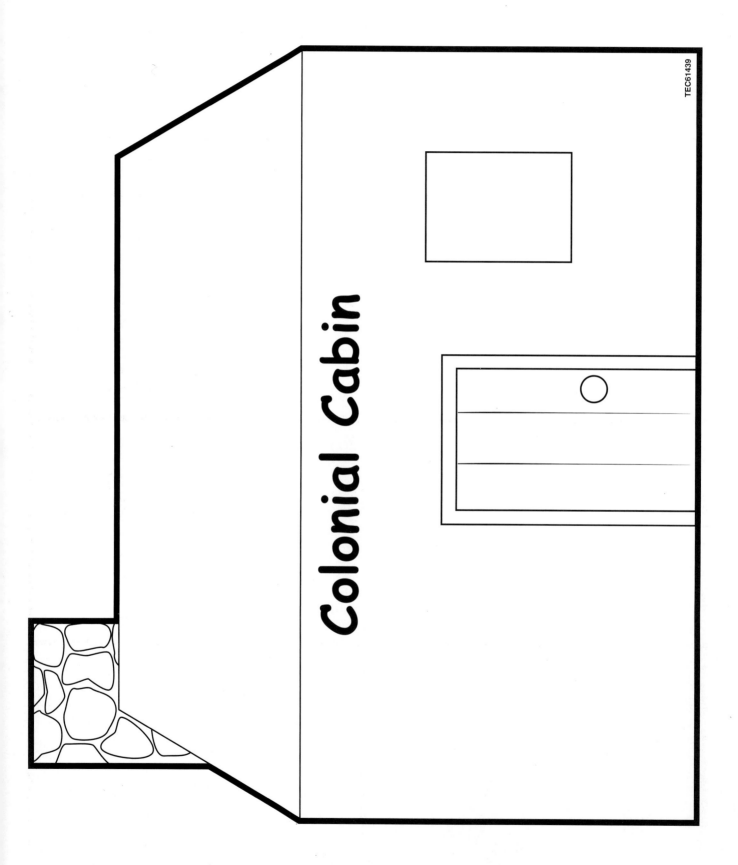

Colonial Cabin

TEC61439

The Busy Teacher's Seasonal Book • ©The Mailbox® Books • TEC61439

Read a hornbook.
TEC61439

Sew a sampler.
TEC61439

Roll a hoop with a stick.
TEC61439

Churn some butter.
TEC61439

Feed the chickens.
TEC61439

Spin a top.
TEC61439

Write with a feather quill.
TEC61439

Fly a kite.
TEC61439

Wrapped Up for the Holidays

ideas contributed by Ada Goren, Winston-Salem, NC

LITERACY

Add a Bow

For this center, use a black marker to write a different color word on each of several paper lunch bags. Place inside each bag a piece of construction paper in the corresponding color. Fold each bag to close it and slide a paper clip onto the fold. Also color a copy of a bow pattern from page 24 to match each bag. Place the bows and bags at a center. A child reads each color word and slides the matching bow under the paper clip. To check her work, she opens the bag to see whether the paper inside matches the bow. **Color words (RF.K.3c)**

red

yellow

green

Editor's Tip:
To keep the bags from easily tipping over, place a small wooden block in each one.

MATH

Gifts Galore

Wrap up lots of learning with activities that are easy to adapt to different skills! To prepare, gather holiday gift wrap in four different designs. Help each child wrap a large wooden block to make a pretend gift. Then use the gifts in the ideas below.

Graphing: Arrange graph labels, like the ones shown, on the floor. In turn, ask each youngster to place his gift in its corresponding graph column. After the object graph is complete, ask students graph-related questions.

Ordinal numbers: Have each child color a unique design on a copy of the bow pattern on page 24. Then have her tape it to her gift. Collect the gifts and line up ten of them. Next, ask ordinal number–related questions, such as, "Which gift has holly paper and a green and yellow bow?"

Patterning: Use some of the gifts to start a pattern. Then ask student volunteers to continue the pattern. For an added challenge, invite students to create patterns for their classmates to continue.

Giving gifts is fun to do.
Here's a gift from me to you.

Giving the Alphabet

These student-made gifts are full of letter practice! To make a gift, have each child fold a sheet of construction paper in half vertically. Then give used magazines and a different letter manipulative to each student. Direct her to cut out pictures of items whose names begin with her letter. Then have her glue the pictures to the inside of her paper. (Collect the letter manipulatives.) Encourage her to decorate the front of her folded paper to resemble a gift.

After students finish making their gifts, invite a child to stand as you lead the class in the rhyme shown to the right. At the end of the rhyme, instruct the child to open her gift and show her classmates. Have students name the pictures and identify their beginning letter. *Letter-sound correspondence (RF.K.3a)*

I made a flower for Grammy.

MATH AND LITERACY

In the Bag

For this center, put a supply of pattern blocks in a gift bag. Place the bag, blank paper, and writing materials at a center. A child arranges the blocks on a sheet of paper to make a gift. He traces the outline of his creation and colors it. Then he writes or dictates a sentence about his gift. *Shapes, writing (K.G.B.6, W.K.3)*

LITERACY

Priceless Presents

Incorporate gift giving and writing! Help youngsters understand that they can give gifts that don't cost money. Enlist students' help in coming up with a list of some of these special gifts, such as giving hugs and helping around the house. Then have each child write or dictate on a sheet of paper a sentence about a gift she would like to give to someone. Have her draw the gift. Then direct her to glue her drawing to a slightly larger sheet of gift wrap. Have her cut out and complete a copy of a gift tag pattern from page 24 and glue it on the gift. Invite students to share their finished projects with the class before giving them to their intended recipients. *Writing (W.K.3)*

This gift is for Mom

I will help set the table.

Gift Bow Patterns
Use with "Add a Bow" and "Gifts Galore" on page 22.

Gift Tag Patterns
Use with "Priceless Presents" on page 23.

This gift is for

This gift is for

Seasonal Skill Practice
Frosty Fun

These science, math, and literacy ideas are just in time for wintry weather!

adapted from ideas contributed by Laurie K. Gibbons, Huntsville, AL

I see snow.

It feels cold.

It gets dark before dinner.

I wear mittens to keep warm.

The trees have no leaves.

I wear a big jacket.

SCIENCE
Chilly Changes

Is the temperature dropping? Do your students feel a chill in the air? Ask youngsters about the changes they see, smell, hear, taste, and feel during the transition from fall to winter. Write each student's response on a white paper circle (snowball) and display the snowballs one above the other to form a tall snowpal body. Then top the body off with a snowpal head. **To extend the activity,** have youngsters use the display to help them write about and illustrate winter-related scenes. *Recognizing seasonal changes*

LITERACY
No School?

If the seasonal conditions closed your school for a day, your students would surely keep busy! Sing this short tune to prompt a discussion of what youngsters might like to do on a snow day. Following the discussion, have each child write to complete the sentence "On a snow day, I would…" Then have her draw a picture to match her writing. *Writing (W.K.3)*

On a snow day, I would go sledding at the park!

(sung to the tune of "Do Your Ears Hang Low?")

If you hear "no school," what would you do that day?
Would you stay inside or go outside to play?
Blankets, boots, and scarves—comfy things that keep you warm
If you hear "no school."

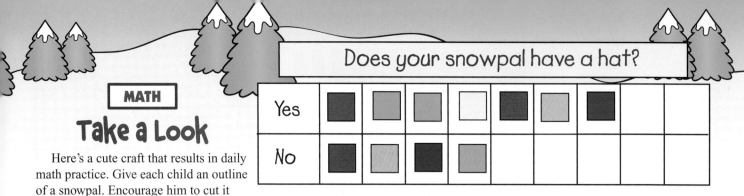

Does your snowpal have a hat?

Yes	■	■	■	□	■	■	■		
No	■	■	■	■					

MATH

Take a Look

Here's a cute craft that results in daily math practice. Give each child an outline of a snowpal. Encourage him to cut it out and add details as desired. Then post a question of the day, such as "Is your snowpal smiling?" Invite each youngster to put a sticky note or paper square on a simple graph to respond yes or no. Discuss the results as time allows. To change the graph, simply remove the squares and post a different question. *Graphing*

Super snowpal! "My" is the winning word.

	my		
	my	see	
the	my	see	can

LITERACY

Super Snowpal!

Your kindergartners are sure to be eager to read and write words at this partner center. In advance, secure a paper clip and brad to a tagboard copy of the spinner pattern on page 27. At a center, put the spinner, a copy of the recording sheet from page 27 for each child, and pencils.

To play, a child spins the spinner and writes the word in the matching column on her recording sheet. Then her partner takes a turn. When a player writes the same word three times, she says, "Super snowpal!" and announces the winning word. If desired, have the twosome continue until one player fills her paper. *High-frequency words (RF.K.3c)*

MATH OR LITERACY

Pockets Full of Snow

These snowpals include storage pockets! For each skill you would like to review, glue a half circle to a snowpal cutout to make a pocket; then label the snowpal's hat with the skill. Next, write on white paper circles (snowballs) numbers, letters, or words, or draw pictures or shapes that correspond with the skill. Slide the snowballs in the snowpal's pocket. If desired, place matching-color dots or stickers on the back of each snowpal and its snowballs for easy sorting. Now it's ready-to-use and easy to transport! *Skill practice*

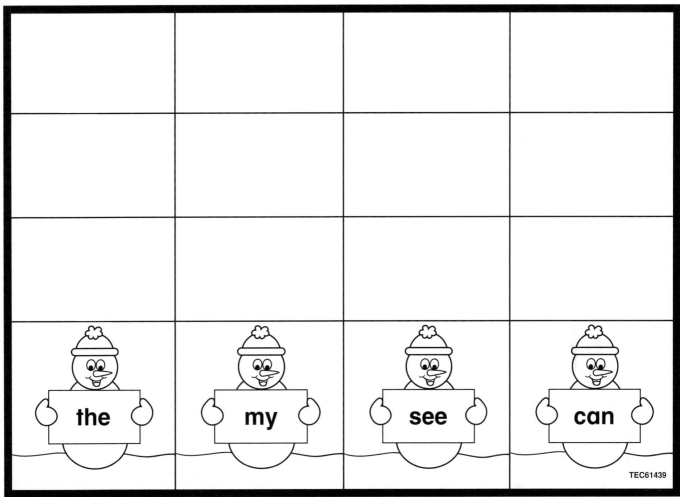

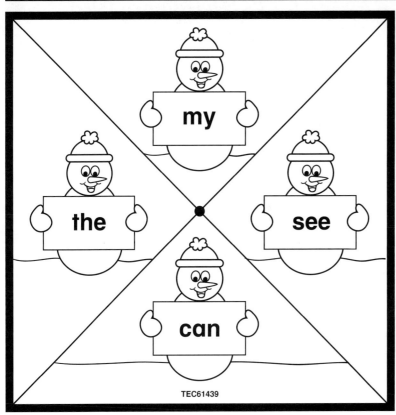

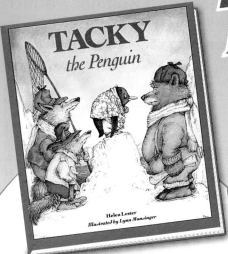

Tacky the Penguin

by Helen Lester

Tacky the penguin is not like his penguin companions. He does not march like them, dive like them, or even sing like them. But it is his unique personality that deters a group of penguin hunters from trapping his friends and him. In the end of this humorous tale, the other penguins realize that even though Tacky is different, he is a very important friend.

ideas contributed by Ada Goren, Winston-Salem, NC

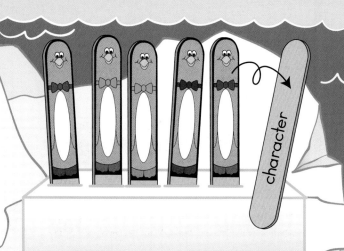

Pick a Penguin

Story elements (RL.K.3)

Add an arctic twist to reviewing the important parts of the story. After youngsters are familiar with the story, glue five copies of the penguin pattern (page 29) to separate large craft sticks. Program the back of each stick with one of the following story elements: *character, setting, event from the beginning, event from the middle,* and *event from the end.* Insert the penguins into a block of white foam or a container filled with rice to make an iceberg. Invite a child to pick a penguin from the iceberg and help him read the stick. Then ask youngsters to identify that story element. After accepting several answers, put the penguin aside and continue with the remaining penguins.

An Extraordinary Bird

Reality and fantasy

Youngsters are sure to find the fantastical things that Tacky does to be entertaining! Guide students to understand that Tacky is a character in a story and does not act like a real penguin. Then help each child fold a 9" x 12" sheet of paper in half and unfold it. Have her cut out a copy of the reality and fantasy penguin cards and strips on page 29. Direct her to glue each penguin card to the top of a different column on her paper. Then help her read each strip and glue it in the correct column.

So Special!

Story theme (RL.K.2)

Tacky is not like his friends, which is why he is unique! After reading the story, ask students to name some things that Tacky does that are different from what his companions do. Lead little ones to conclude that everyone is special in her own way. Then give each child two shirt cutouts. Have her decorate one shirt as desired. On the other shirt, encourage her to draw, write, or dictate something special about herself. To complete the project, help her place the decorated shirt atop the other shirt and staple them together as shown. Then help her cut through the middle of the top shirt. Encourage each child to share her unique project with the class.

I am special because I play soccer.

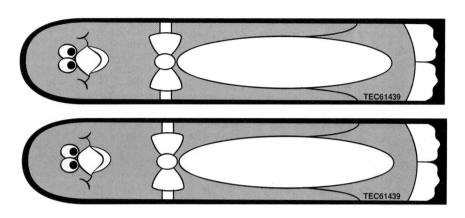

Reality and Fantasy Penguin Cards and Strips
Use with "An Extraordinary Bird" on page 28.

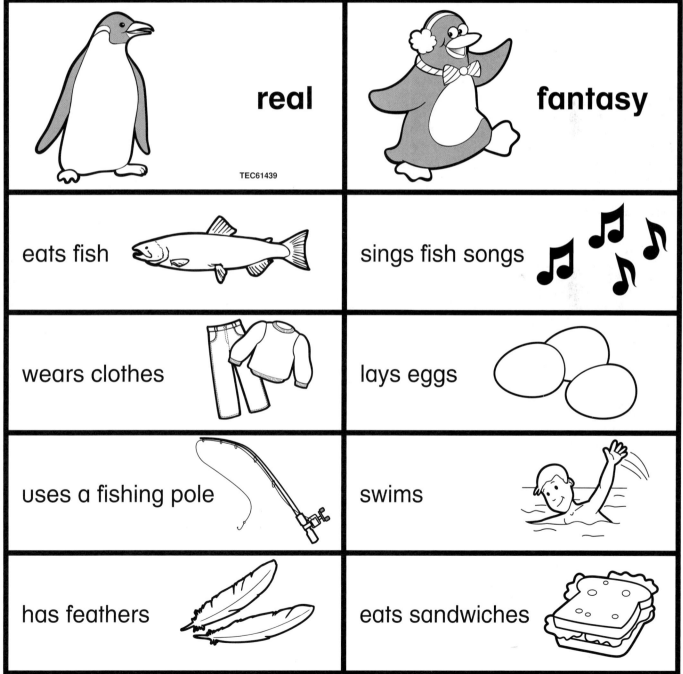

real

fantasy

eats fish

sings fish songs

wears clothes

lays eggs

uses a fishing pole

swims

has feathers

eats sandwiches

Let's Celebrate the 100th Day

A Number Lineup

Matching numbers, number order

Number 100 sticky dots from 1 to 100. Attach each dot to a small object and store the objects in a container. Place a number line from 1 to 100 on the floor and set the container nearby. Have a child take an object, find the matching number on the number line, and place the object below the number. Have students take turns until all the objects are correctly placed.

Jody Carlson
Smith Elementary
Berea, OH

Editor's Tip:
If you don't have a number line to 100, attach a long strip of masking tape to the floor and write the numbers on it.

Dear Family,
Our class will be celebrating the 100th day of school on _January 11_. Please have your child put 100 of the same object in the paper bag. Then help him/her write three clues about the object. Please return the bag and clues on 100th Day. Thanks for your help.

Sam _name_ 's Clues
1. They are soft.
2. They are white.
3. They look like a bunny's tail.

Three Clues

Counting, critical thinking

Prior to the 100th day of school, send home with each child a paper lunch bag and a copy of the note at the top of page 32. Invite a family member to help the child place 100 like objects in the bag, write three clues about the objects, and return the note and bag to school. On 100th Day, encourage the child to share his clues. Then choose volunteers to name what they think is in the bag. **For an added challenge,** later in the day, direct each child to arrange and count his items in sets of ten.

Blythe Purdin, Rockport Elementary, Rockport, MA

Chicks Aplenty
Counting, tally marks

Prior to the 100th day of school, have youngsters decorate yellow paper ovals to make 100 chicks like the one shown. On 100th Day, hide the chicks around the room before students arrive. To begin the activity, read aloud *The Wolf's Chicken Stew* by Keiko Kasza and then invite youngsters to find the chicks. Next, make a tally chart to count the chicks found. Lead students in counting the tallies. If all 100 chicks have not been found, help students determine how many chicks are missing. Then invite youngsters to find the remaining chicks. If desired, display the chicks for an eye-catching reminder of 100th Day and the value of teamwork!

Suzi Boyett, Harney Elementary, Lebanon, IN

31. Julius   36. Keida
32. Donovan   37. Anna
33. Kara   38. Steve
34. Elise   39.
35. Jake   40.

An Autograph Collection
Counting, writing

Number ten half sheets of paper from 1 to 100, putting ten numbers on each sheet. For each child, staple a copy of the sheets between two half sheets of construction paper. Have each child personalize a copy of the cover at the bottom of page 32 and glue it to the front of his book. Next, read aloud the poem on the cover and have each child sign his name in his book. During the day, encourage students to ask their classmates, teachers, and students in other classes to write their names in his book. At the end of the day, direct him to count the number of autographs he has collected. If his book has fewer than 100 signatures, encourage him to take it home and collect the remaining signatures from family and friends.

Jodi Darter, Cabool Elementary, Cabool, MO

Hop to 100
Counting by tens

For this center activity, program each of ten large construction paper squares as shown. Laminate the squares for durability and tape them to the floor to form a hopscotch board. To count by tens to 100, a child hops on the board and names the numbers.

Susan Miller Geisler
Oakmont Elementary
Fort Worth, TX

Dear Family,
   Our class will be celebrating the 100th day of school on
_____. Please have your child put 100 of
the same object in the paper bag. Then help him/her write three
clues about the object. Please return the bag and clues on 100th
Day. Thanks for your help.

's Clues

_____
                name

1. _____

2. _____

3. _____

TEC61439

's Autograph Book

_____

Today is the 100th Day.

Hip hip hooray!

I'm collecting autographs all day.

There are 100 places for people to sign.

Make that 99—one place is mine!

TEC61439

Note to the teacher: Use the top half of the page with "Three Clues" on page 30. Use the bottom half of the page with "An Autograph Collection" on page 31.

The Busy Teacher's Seasonal Book • ©The Mailbox® Books • TEC61439

Just for Valentine's Day!

♥ How Many Hearts?

Candy hearts add festive flair to nonstandard measurement. Make available a supply of candy hearts and several small classroom items. Encourage each youngster to use the hearts to measure each item. Then have him record his measurements on a sheet like the one shown. *adapted from an idea by Rebecca L. Mueller, Clay Road Baptist School, Houston, TX*

Name Scott	
What I measured	♥ hearts
✏️	8
✋	6
🅰️	3

♥ Valentine Headbands

After each student opens her valentines, ask her to choose five of her favorites. Have her glue the chosen cards to a construction paper headband. Invite students to wear their headbands during Valentine's Day celebrations. *Joe Appleton, Durham, NC*

♥ Sight Word Placemats

RF.K.3c

To make a placemat, have each child write a different word on each of ten heart cutouts. Then direct him to glue the hearts to a 12" x 18" sheet of construction paper labeled with his name. Laminate the resulting placemats for durability. If desired, invite students to use the placemats when eating Valentine's Day treats. *Felice Kestenbaum, Goosehill Primary, Cold Spring Harbor, NY*

♥ Heart Lotto

RF.K.1d

For this game, give each child a paper strip, five different-color crayons, and five game markers. Have him write "HEART" on his strip, using a different color for each letter. In a bag, place a set of the crayons and letter cards to spell "HEART." To play, remove a crayon and a letter from the bag. If a child has the matching set on his card, he covers it with a marker. Return the items to the bag and play until a child covers all five letters and announces, "I have heart!" *adapted from an idea by Brenda Pritchett, Columbus, MS*

♥ Party Game

Have students sit in a circle. Then stand in front of a child and say, "Oh, sweet friend of mine, will you be my valentine?" as you hand the child a heart cutout. After the child responds, "Yes, I will be your valentine!" the youngster trades places with you. Then she repeats the process with another student. *Marla Cobb, Barhitte Elementary, Burton, MI*

♥ A Happy Hunt

CCSS

Label a class supply of red and pink heart cutouts each with a different number. Secretly hide the hearts around the classroom; then invite each child to find one. After the hunt, use the hearts to reinforce a math skill such as ordering numbers, comparing numbers, or patterning. *Milisa McDaniel, Eshelman Avenue Elementary, Lomita, CA*

Hooray for Dr. Seuss!

Delightful, charming, entertaining, and just plain silly—Dr. Seuss books are pure fun! Use these ideas to inspire youngsters to read here, there, and everywhere!

Tap That Hat!

Rhyming

Does the Cat in the Hat have a favorite hat? Of course he does! So add a fun twist to your rhyming review by encouraging youngsters to wear their favorite hats. Have each child bring a hat of her choice to school. (Glue a tagboard copy of the hat pattern on page 36 to a paper headband for each student who does not have a hat.) After reading a Dr. Seuss story aloud, lead students in one of the options below.

Recognizing rhymes (RF.K.2a): Name pairs of words from the story, most of which rhyme. Instruct each child to touch his hat when he hears two words that rhyme.

Generating rhymes (RF.K.2a): Name a real or nonsense word from the story. Then invite youngsters, in turn, to produce rhyming words. For each correct word, have each child tap her hat!

Reading -*at* words (RF.K.3): Write -*at* on chart paper. Then name words, some of which end with the featured rime. For each matching word, instruct students to tap their hats. Then solicit student help to write each matching word on the chart. For each rhyming word added, read the rhyming word list.

Gerri Primak, Charlotte, NC

-at
hat
cat
mat

Fish.

one   fish
two   here
red   there
blue   everywhere
black   some

See the **practice sheet** on page 37.

Look in a Book

High-frequency words (RF.K.3c)

Dr. Seuss books are not only fun but they also include many words your kindergartners can read! In advance, post a list of high-frequency words from a selected story on a large book cutout. For added interest, have youngsters make Seuss-style characters to embellish the display. Then encourage each child to look and listen for the posted words as you read the story aloud. Each time a word is recognized, have him form silly glasses around his eyes with his fingers. **For a writing activity,** have each youngster write three words from the display and then draw a smiley face next to the corresponding word each time he sees it in the book.

Gerri Primak

So Many Stripes!

Word families (RF.K.3d)

On a wall? In the hall? Show your enthusiasm for reading and writing with these Seuss-style hats! Give each youngster a red copy of the hat pattern on page 36 and four 1" x 6" white paper strips. Assign each student a rime and have him write it on his hat rim. Then, on each strip, instruct him to write a different word that corresponds with the rime. When his words are approved, have him glue the strips to his hat. Then display the completed hats with the rhyme shown.

> We can spell! Yes, it's true!
> Read the words we wrote for you!

Steven Lamkin, Salisbury Christian School, Salisbury, MD

hop
mop
top
shop

-op

jug
mug
rug
bug

-ug

5, 10, 15

The FOOT BOOK By Dr. Seuss

Sarah has blue feet.

How Many Feet?

The Foot Book is easy to adapt for a variety of math and literacy skills. Try one or all of these activities after reading this popular story aloud.

Nonstandard measurement: Set out manipulatives, such as counters, Unifix cubes, and paper clips. Have each child tape a 12-inch length of string to a sheet of paper. Then direct him to choose a manipulative and measure how many it takes to equal one foot. Have him record the information on his paper. Then encourage him to measure with different objects as time permits.

adapted from an idea by Amanda Bangert, Trinity Lutheran School
Grand Island, NE

Counting by fives and tens: Invite youngsters to stand for a Seuss-stomp! Discuss with youngsters how one foot has five toes and two feet have ten toes. Then have students count by fives as they stomp, one foot at a time, around the room. For the next round, have students hop on both feet as they count by tens.

Reading fluency (RF.K.4): Set out different-color paints and help each youngster make her footprints on a sheet of paper. Then have her write on her paper to complete the sentence "[Student name] has [color] feet." When the pages are dry, bind them together between construction paper covers and put the book in your reading area.

So Funny!

Responding to a story

Silly Seuss scenes are sure to prompt some laughter! Before reading a Dr. Seuss book aloud, tell students that, at the end of the story, you will ask them to name the funniest parts of the story. Remind youngsters to listen carefully and look closely at the illustrations. After reading, invite each student to tell which part she thought was the silliest. Then have her write a sentence similar to the one shown and draw a picture to match. **To make a class book,** bind the pages between construction paper covers and add the title "So Funny!" Then invite each youngster to read her page aloud.

Gerri Primak, Charlotte, NC

I laughed when the elephant was pulling the sled!

Hat Pattern
Use with "Tap That Hat!" on page 34 and "So Many Stripes!" on page 35.

TEC61439

The Busy Teacher's Seasonal Book • ©The Mailbox® Books • TEC61439

Color That Hat!

 Read.
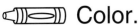 Write.
Color.

Hint: Match the size of the letters and boxes.

Word Bank

Where	see
is	you
have	want

1. I [ ][ ][ ] a blue hat.

2. [ ][ ] [ ][ ][ ] is the red hat?

3. I [ ][ ][ ][ ] a purple hat.

4. The hat [ ][ ] green.

5. Do [ ][ ][ ] see the orange hat?

6. I [ ][ ][ ][ ] a yellow hat.

Bonus: Write a sentence with the words **brown hat.** Draw.

End of the Rainbow

This colorful collection of ideas gives you golden opportunities to reinforce science, math, and literacy skills.

Wonder and Learn
Graphic organizer

Spark students' curiosity with this eye-catching version of a KWL chart. On a length of white bulletin board paper, draw a rainbow extending from a cloud to a pot of gold. Title the three parts of the illustration as shown and then display the resulting poster. To begin, invite youngsters to tell what they know about rainbows. Note the information on the cloud. Next, guide students to ask questions about the topic. Write the questions on or around the rainbow. Over a few days, share relevant nonfiction books, such as *All the Colors of the Rainbow* by Allan Fowler. Then prompt students to recall what they have learned and complete the poster with the information.

adapted from an idea by
Andrea Singleton
Waynesville Elementary
Waynesville, OH

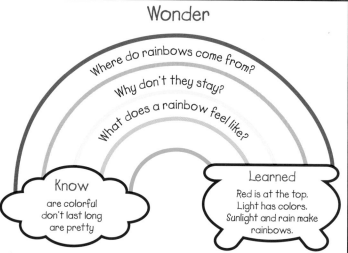

Wonder

Where do rainbows come from?
Why don't they stay?
What does a rainbow feel like?

Know
are colorful
don't last long
are pretty

Learned
Red is at the top.
Light has colors.
Sunlight and rain make rainbows.

Look!
Science

Your students are sure to be surprised to learn that a CD contains a rainbow! Gather an old CD and a flashlight. Give each student a sheet of paper and have her draw a line down the center of it. Next, remind students that scientists are careful observers. Show them the CD and ask each youngster to draw and describe it on the first half of her paper. After each student completes her work, dim the lights and shine the flashlight on the CD at an angle so that rainbow colors appear on a wall. Invite students to describe what they see. Then turn the lights on and have each student record her observations on the second half of her paper. Afterward, tell students that light is made of different colors. Explain that the CD helps make the colors visible much like rain sometimes makes the colors in sunlight visible.

Emile Blake, Sherrills Ford Elementary, Sherrills Ford, NC

In the Clouds
Phonics (RF.K.3b)

What words have the long *a* sound as in *rain* and *rainbow?* That's the question students explore with this pocket chart activity. To prepare, illustrate and label a strip of paper to make a heading similar to the one shown. (If appropriate for your students, label the second cloud "Short *a.*") Display the heading in the top row of a pocket chart. Cut out the picture cards on page 40 and back them with tagboard for durability. Shuffle the cards and then stack them facedown.

To complete the activity, have a volunteer take the top card and name the picture. If the word has a long *a* sound, his classmates give a thumbs-up. If it does not have a long *a* sound, they give a thumbs-down. The volunteer places the card below the correct cloud. Students sort the remaining cards in the same manner and then name the pictures in each group. **For more advanced students,** have youngsters match word cards to the sorted pictures and then study the vowel patterns.

Golden Coin Toss
Math or reading

For this easy-to-adapt activity, cover two cardboard circles with gold foil to make coins. To make a floor mat, divide a large piece of paper into 12 sections and color them as shown. Choose an option below and program 12 blank cards as described. Then attach a different card to each section. (Use reusable adhesive to allow for later reprogramming.) Place the mat on the floor and have students take turns as described below.

Addition: Program the cards with various numbers, writing one number per card. To play, a youngster tosses both coins onto the mat. She reads the numbers in the sections where the coins landed and then announces their sum.

High-frequency words (RF.K.3c): Write a different word on each card. To play, a youngster tosses a coin onto the mat. She spells the corresponding word and then the group names it.

Andrea Singleton, Waynesville Elementary
Waynesville, OH

Picture Cards

Use with "In the Clouds" on page 39.

TEC61439

TEC61439

TEC61439

TEC61439

TEC61439

TEC61439

TEC61439

TEC61439

TEC61439

TEC61439

TEC61439

TEC61439

Seasonal Skill Practice
Showers and Flowers

When it rains literacy, math, and science, your youngsters are sure to bloom!

SCIENCE

From Root to Flower

Teach students this song to help them remember the parts of a plant and the order in which they grow. While singing the song, post a copy of the cards from page 43. If desired, give each child a copy of the cards to manipulate while singing. *Parts of a plant*

(sung to the tune of "Head and Shoulders")

Roots, stem, leaves, and flowers make a plant.
Roots, stem, leaves, and flowers make a plant.
This is the order in which a plant grows.
Roots, stem, leaves, and flowers make a plant!

Jenn Daub
St. John the Baptist Catholic School
Longmont, CO

MATH

Raindrops and Roses

Rain showers make beautiful roses grow at this center. Program a sheet of paper with the sentence shown; then copy it to make a class supply. At a center, place the papers, blue and red washable ink pads, and a green marker. A child makes blue raindrop prints and red rose prints (using the green marker to draw stems) on her paper. When she is satisfied with her work, she counts the flowers and raindrops and then completes the sentence.
Comparing sets (K.CC.C.6)

Angie Kutzer
Garrett Elementary
Mebane, NC

There are more [🌼] than [🖐].

SCIENCE
To the Top!

Before introducing this partner game, guide students to understand that in order for most seeds to grow into plants, they need water, soil, air, and light. Brainstorm with youngsters different ways that a seed meets its needs, such as getting light from the sun or a lamp and getting water from rain or a hose.

To prepare for the game, give each twosome a copy of page 44 and two game markers. After the partners cut out the cards and gameboards and stack the cards facedown, have each partner take a gameboard. To play, each player places his marker on his gameboard's seed. The first player takes a card and, if the card shows something that helps a seed grow into a plant, he moves his game marker up one space along the stem. If it is an item that a seed does not need, he sets the card aside and his turn is over. Players reshuffle the cards as needed. Alternate play continues until one child reaches the flower. *Basic needs of a plant*

Angie Kutzer, Garrett Elementary, Mebane, NC

MATH
Flower Arrangements

To prepare for this center, program cards with different addition problems. Place at a center the cards, a vase cutout, flower blossoms (large pom-poms or flower cutouts) in two different colors, and paper. A student places a card on the vase and then places flowers above the vase to model the addition problem. After writing the number sentence on a sheet of paper, she removes the flowers and card and plays again. *Addition (K.OA.A.1)*

Angie Kutzer

Editor's Tip:
Set out green pipe cleaners for youngsters to use as flower stems.

LITERACY
The Shower Shuffle

Youngsters pretend to be raindrops in this whole-group activity. To prepare, program a class supply of raindrop cutouts (patterns on page 43) with words from three different word families. (Repeat words as needed.) Draw three clouds on the board and label each one with one of the chosen word families. To begin, give each youngster a raindrop and have students gather together to form a rain cloud. Then clap your hands to represent a rain shower. As you clap, students disperse and each child lines up behind the cloud with the matching word family. After each student reads her word, collect and then redistribute the raindrops to prepare for another shower! **For independent practice,** place the raindrops and labeled cloud cutouts at a center. *Word families (RF.K.3)*

Angie Kutzer

See page 45 for a **skill sheet** on word families.

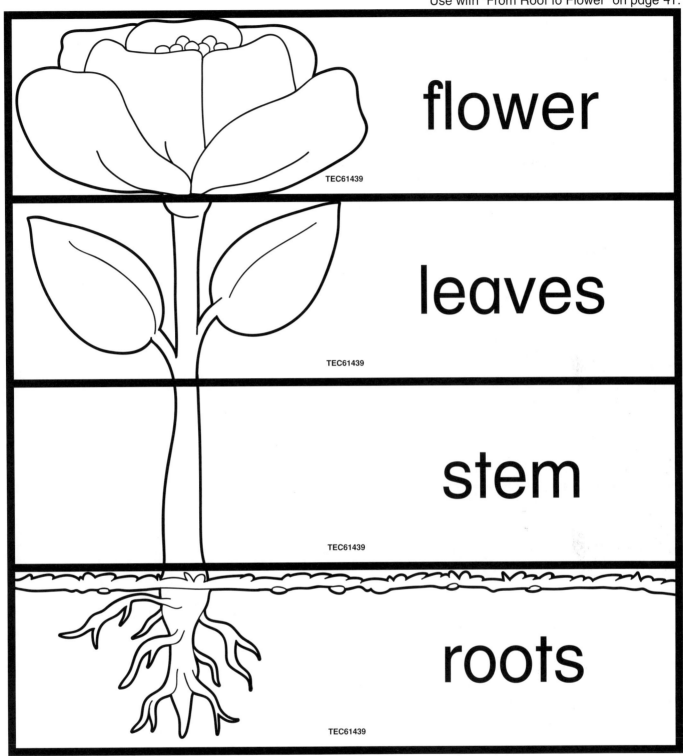

flower

TEC61439

leaves

TEC61439

stem

TEC61439

roots

TEC61439

Raindrop Patterns
Use with "The Shower Shuffle" on page 42.

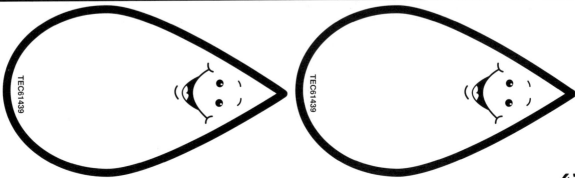

TEC61439

TEC61439

Gameboards and Game Cards

Use with "To the Top!" on page 42.

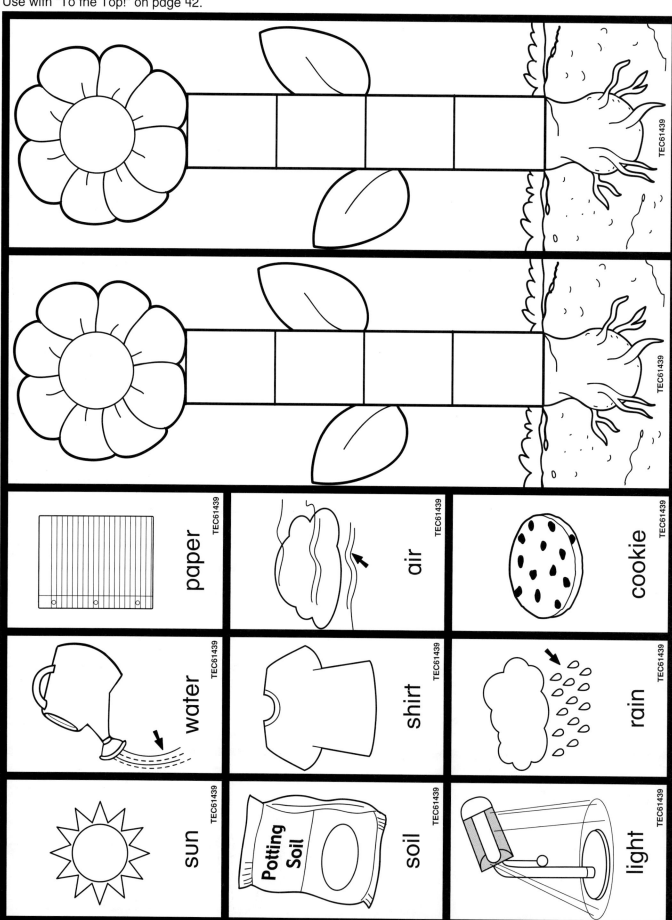

paper

air

cookie

water

shirt

rain

sun

Potting Soil

soil

light

Drip, Drop!

 Write **ip** or **op** to make each word.

ip
as in ship

op
as in mop

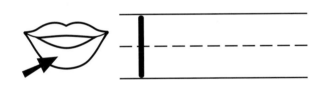 l

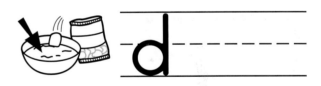 d

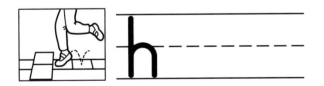 h

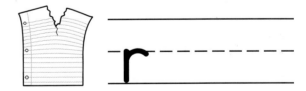 r

 ch

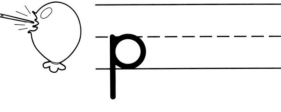 p

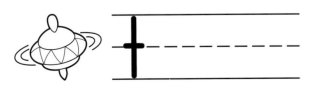 t

 ch

Seasonal Skill Practice
Bugs

ideas contributed by Laurie K. Gibbons, Huntsville, AL

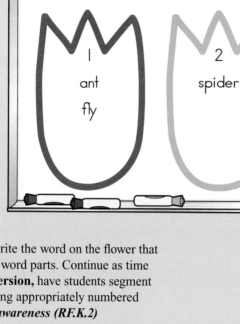

1
ant
fly

2
spider

3
butterfly

LITERACY

Finding Flowers

Youngsters pretend to be butterflies during this whole-group activity. In advance, draw three flowers on the board and number them. To begin, announce a word that has one, two, or three syllables. Lead students to repeat the word as they "flap their wings" like butterflies once for each word part. Then write the word on the flower that corresponds with the number of word parts. Continue as time allows. **For a more advanced version,** have students segment words into individual sounds using appropriately numbered flower drawings. ***Phonological awareness (RF.K.2)***

head

abdomen   thorax

                           antenna

wing   leg

Game mat

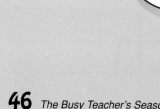

Name __Parker__

Build a Bug

SCIENCE

Build a Bug

Reinforce the parts of a bug with a small-group game. Add a brad and a paper clip to a tagboard copy of the spinner on page 48 as shown. Give each child in the group a copy of the game mat on page 48. In turn, each youngster spins the spinner, identifies the body part, and colors a matching part on his game mat. If the body part is already colored, his turn is over. Play continues until one student has all the body parts colored. ***Parts of an insect***

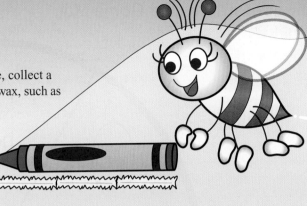

Made by Bees!

Bees are the inspiration for this measurement activity. In advance, collect a variety of products that are made by bees or can be made from beeswax, such as honey, candles, crayons, shoe polish, or lipstick. Also cut yellow pipe cleaners into one-inch pieces to make a supply of bees. Have students use the bees to measure the lengths of the different items. Then ask each child to choose two items and compare the lengths. **For more advanced students,** have them write and draw to show how two items compare to each other. *Nonstandard measurement*

LITERACY OR MATH

Bug Jars

For this center activity, cut from construction paper several jar shapes and a supply of ladybugs. Then program the jars and bugs as described in an option below.

Addition (K.OA.A.1): Program each of three jars with a different sum. Then label each ladybug with an addition problem and matching dot sets. A child solves the problem on each ladybug and places the ladybug on the jar with the matching sum.

Number words (RF.K.3c): Program each of ten jars with a different number word. Then label the ladybugs with the numerals 1–10. A student places each ladybug on the jar with the matching number word.

Letters (RF.K.1d): Draw a happy face on one jar and a sad face on another. Then label each ladybug with an uppercase and lowercase letter, making sure that some are matching pairs and some are not. A child places correct letter pairs on the happy face and incorrect ones on the sad face. **For an added challenge,** he rewrites each incorrect pair to make it correct.

LITERACY

Busy Bugs

This writing activity doubles as a unique display! Enlist students' help in compiling a list of bug-themed action words. On a white paper strip, have each child write and illustrate a sentence about a bug using one of the listed words. Next, have her glue her strip to the center of a slightly larger piece of black construction paper. After each child has completed her project, punch holes along the top and bottom of each paper. Display the papers in rows to look like a film strip and add the title shown. *Action words (L.K.1b)*

Spinner Pattern and Game Mat
Use with "Build a Bug" on page 46.

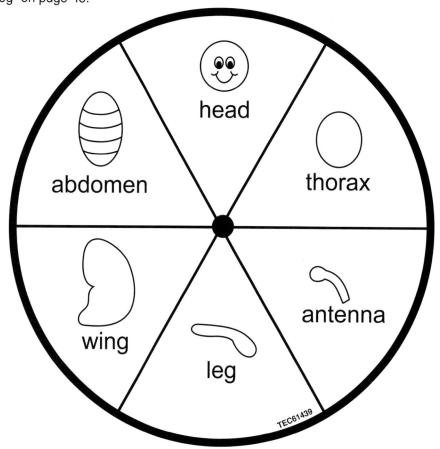

abdomen

head

thorax

wing

leg

antenna

TEC61439

- -

Name _____ Game mat

Build a Bug

"Toad-ally" Cool Year-End Ideas

From expressing gratitude to making a summer reading list, students are sure to enjoy hopping toward the last day of school with these activities!

ideas contributed by Laurie K. Gibbons, Huntsville, AL

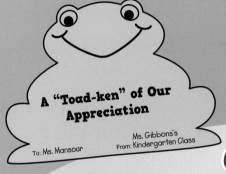

A "Toad-ken" of Our Appreciation

To: Ms. Mansour
From: Ms. Gibbons's Kindergarten Class

June 2014
Ms. Mansour,
Your dedication to literature and our school library has helped us grow by leaps and bounds! Thank you for all you do!

B.J. liked the way you read the stories.

Green With Gratitude!

Help youngsters express appreciation to support staff and parent volunteers with these **thank-you booklets**! To make one, cut out a green copy of the booklet cover on page 51. Use the front cover as a tracer to make a back cover and a class supply of student pages. Personalize the front cover and share it with your youngsters. Then guide each child to complete a page by drawing and writing about something the recipient did or shared, such as a favorite book from the media specialist, a favorite song with the music teacher, or a skill-related task with a volunteer. If desired, write a thank-you note on an extra page to tell how the person helped your class grow by leaps and bounds this school year. Then bind the completed pages between the covers.

"Un-frog-ettable" Memories

_____Katie_____'s
Kindergarten Memories
2013–2014

Years from now, preserved kindergarten moments in this **time capsule** are sure to be appreciated. Collect cardboard tubes or canisters to have a class supply. For each child, personalize and sign a copy of the note on page 52. Then guide each student to complete a copy of page 53. Using the options below, prepare other materials to include in each capsule. After each child puts her capsule items in her tube, help her wrap the tube in brown paper so it resembles a log and label it as shown. Then have her use craft materials to make a frog and glue it to her log. Now that's an "un-frog-ettable" keepsake!

Time Capsule Options

Note from the teacher	Writing samples
Kindergarten questionnaire	Artwork
School news	Self-portrait
Class newsletter	Painted handprints
Piece of string that shows	Class photo
child's current height	

Our "Toad-ally" Cool Class

Sarah Isaac Liam Jessica Felipe
Juan Monica Tyler Evan
Peter Matthew Kate Danny Carrie

2013–2014

Fashionable Friends

These **class-made T-shirts** not only serve as kindergarten keepsakes but are also perfect for end-of-the-year programs, award ceremonies, and the last day of school! For each student, obtain a plain white or light blue T-shirt and label it with a title and academic year as shown. Put a piece of cardboard inside each shirt to separate the front and back of the shirt. Guide each child to use a permanent marker to write her name in small letters on the front of each shirt. Also have her use green or brown fabric paint to make a fingerprint above her name. When the paint is dry, help each child draw eyes and a mouth to transform her fingerprint into a toad.

Editor's Tip:
As an alternative, make one class T-shirt and put it on a stuffed animal to serve as an end-of-the-year mascot.

Getting a Jump on Summer!

Students hop, skip, and jump as they countdown to the last day of school with this **display idea**! Write each number from 1 to 10 on a separate lily pad cutout. On the back of each one, write an exercise of your choice. Display the lily pads on a pond background with the title shown, leaving a space by the last lily pad. On the appropriate day, post a frog cutout by the number 10 lily pad to begin the countdown. Then flip the lily pad and have youngsters perform the programmed action. At the end of the last day of school, post blue tissue paper to represent the frog's splash as it hops into summer! **For a skill-related variation**, program the back of each lily pad with a review question for youngsters to answer.

Splash Into Summer!

I like the Frog and Toad books.

Ribbit, Read It!

Select an option from the ideas below to motivate **summer reading**!

- **Personal reading list:** Make a copy of the recording sheet on page 52. Instruct each child to record ten books he reads (or listens to) over the summer. If desired, offer a small reward, such as a new pencil, for completed papers returned in the fall.

- **Home-school connection:** Invite youngsters to share their favorite book titles and give a brief description of what makes the story appealing. Write each title on a chart. Then lead students to select a top ten list of favorites. Transfer the list to a copy of the recording sheet on page 52 and make a class supply. Encourage each child to share the list with her family and use it to find interesting, age-appropriate books to read during the summer.

To:

From:

A "Toad-ken" of Our Appreciation

TEC61439

Dear _____,

I still remember greeting you

On your first day of school.

We spent that first week learning

The routines and all the rules.

The months flew by, we learned and laughed,

And we had a lot of fun!

Soon the year was over,

Though it seemed it had just begun.

Congratulations and Best Wishes!

Note to the teacher: Use with "'Un-frog-ettable' Memories" on page 49.

Name _____

Read It!

1. _____

2. _____

3. _____

4. _____

5. _____

6. _____

7. _____

8. _____

9. _____

10. _____

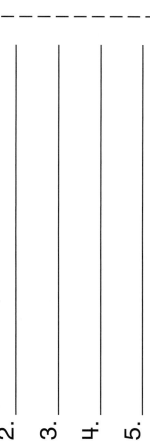 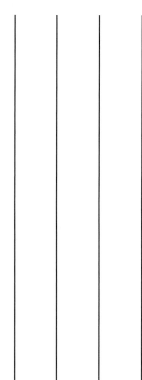  

52

Note to the teacher: Use with "Ribbit, Read It!" on page 50.

_____'s

Kindergarten Memories

Favorite Food

At school, I liked to

_____

_____

_____

_____

I am glad I learned

_____

_____

_____

Favorite Food

More about me:

_____

_____

_____

The Busy Teacher's Seasonal Book • ©The Mailbox® Books • TEC61439

Note to the teacher: Use with "'Un-frog-ettable' Memories" on page 49.

Along the Stem

Counting (K.CC.B.5)

This sunny center provides practice with making number sets. Number ten sunflower cutouts (patterns on page 58) from 1 to 10. Then tape a green pipe cleaner stem to each flower and put the sunflowers in a plastic vase. Place the vase and ten leaf cutouts at a center. A child takes a sunflower, reads the number, and puts the matching number of leaves along the stem. She checks her work by recounting the leaves; then she removes the leaves and takes another flower.

Marie E. Cecchini, West Dundee, IL

On the Go

High-frequency words (RF.K.3c)

On each of several vehicle cutouts (patterns on page 59) write a different high-frequency word, being sure to match the number of letters in the word to the number of windows on the vehicle. Place the vehicles at a center along with letter tiles and paper. A child takes a vehicle and reads the word. Then she places a letter on each window to spell the word. After she writes the word on her paper, she removes the letters and repeats the process with another vehicle.

Sheri Wallace
Ed White Elementary
Eldridge, IA

If You Take a Cat to Beale Elementary...

All Around the School

Making a class book (L.I.1f)

First-day jitters are sure to disappear with this literature-based activity! Read aloud *If You Take a Mouse to School* by Laura Numeroff. Then show students a small stuffed animal. Ask them to imagine what it could do in different parts of the school. Next, take the animal and a camera on a school tour with students. Photograph the animal in various locations and with different staff members. Later, mount each photograph on a separate sheet of paper and add a student-generated caption. Then bind the papers between two covers to make a class book.

Brenda Saunders, Beale Elementary
Gallipolis Ferry, OH

A Welcoming Song

Name recognition

Greet each student with this catchy tune that also reinforces name recognition. Write each child's name on a separate card and store the cards in a bag. To begin, draw a card and display it for the class. Encourage the child whose name is displayed to stand as you lead the class in singing the song shown. Continue until the group has sung to each student.

Deborah Hembrook
Lowell School
Waukesha, WI

(sung to the tune of "Are You Sleeping?")

Welcome, [child's name],
Welcome, [child's name],
To our class,
To our class.
We're so glad you came here.
We're so glad you came here.
Let's be friends.
Let's be friends.

Editor's Tip:
This song is great for welcoming students who join the class later in the year!

In advance, take a photo of each child and trim a circle around her head. Have each student color a copy of the rocket ship on page 60. Then have her glue her photo and tissue paper flames to her rocket as shown. Display the projects along with glittery star cutouts.

Felice Kestenbaum, Jericho, NY

This unique display is sure to receive plenty of compliments! Cut pockets from pairs of jeans, keeping the pockets attached to the material. Then use puff fabric paint to label the pockets with different job names. Mount the pockets on a wall and add flower cutouts, if desired. To use the display, simply place a personalized jumbo craft stick in each pocket to assign a student to each job.

Karri Ann Hraban, St. Teresa School, Lincoln, NE

Pack for School

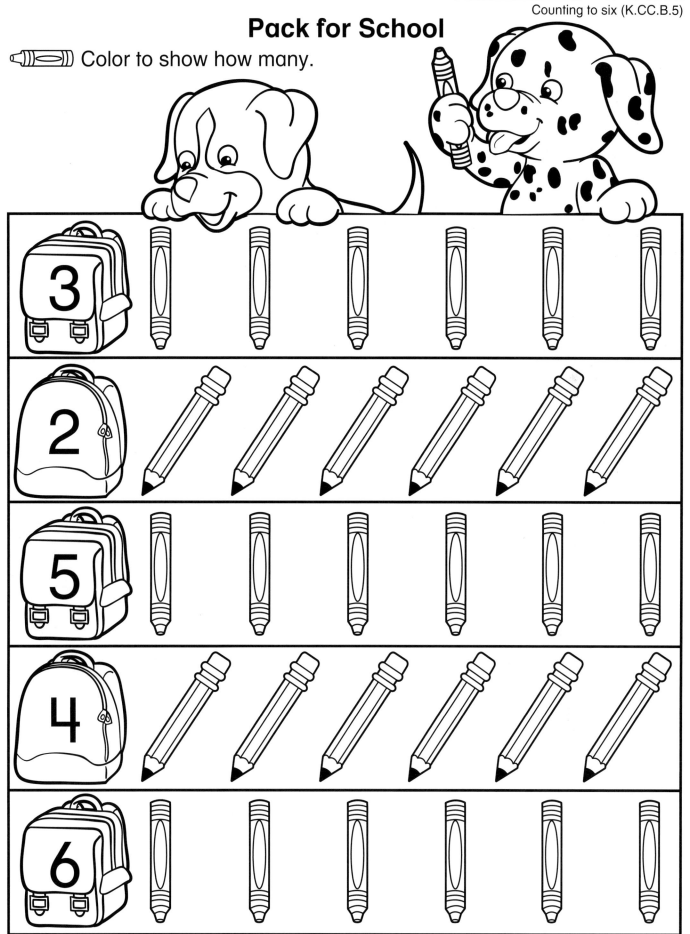

Color to show how many.

Sunflower Patterns

Use with "Along the Stem" on page 54.

TEC61439

TEC61439

TEC61439

TEC61439

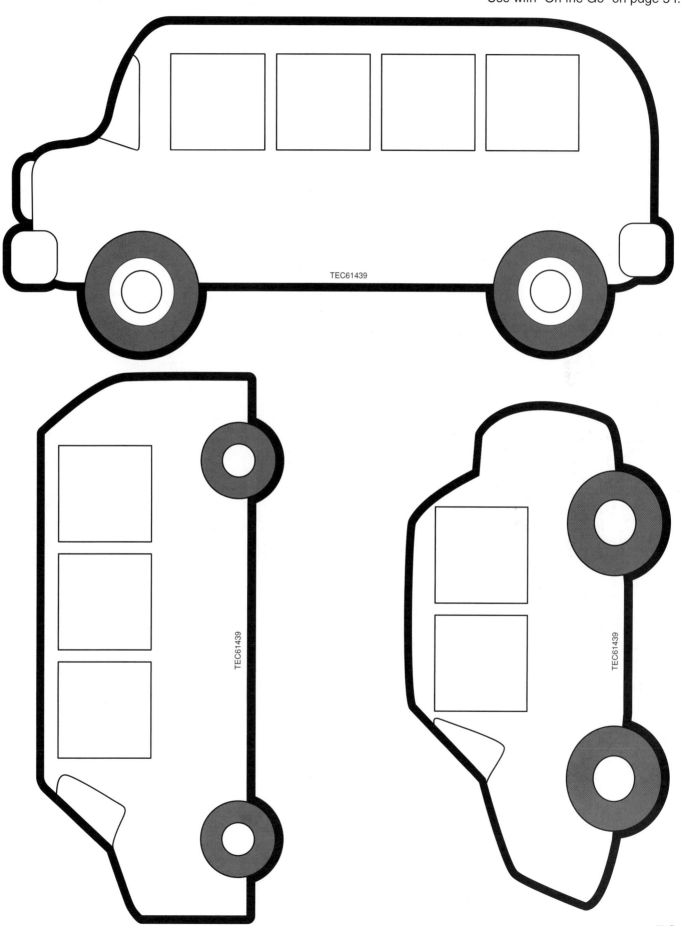

TEC61439

TEC61439

TEC61439

Rocket Ship Pattern

Use with "Blast Off Into Kindergarten!" on page 56.

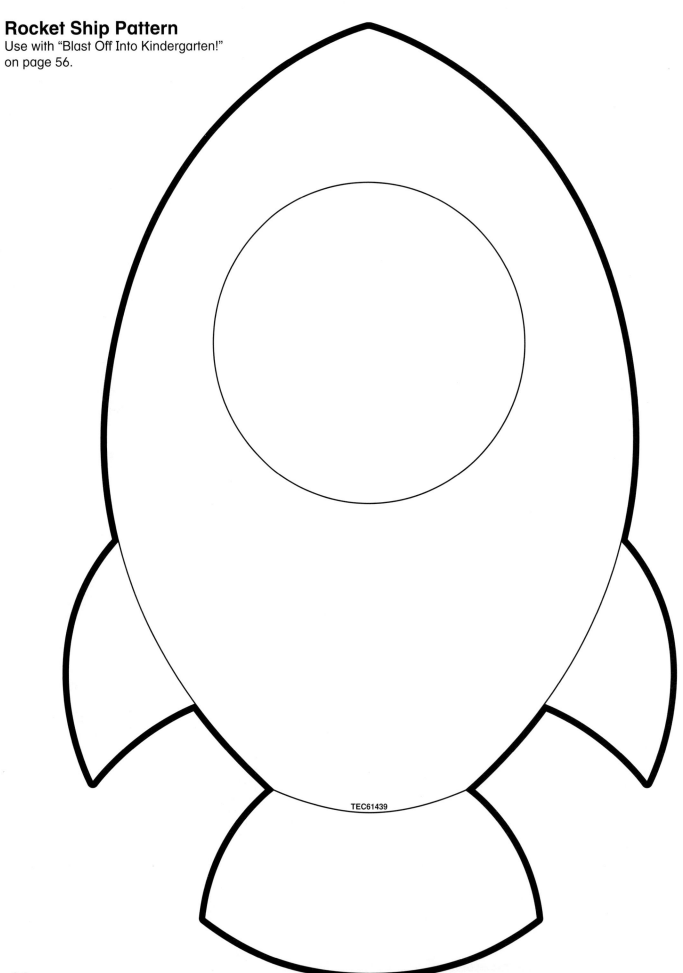

TEC61439

SEPTEMBER

Little worm, little worm,
Look and see.
Pick your apple
From the tree.

Apples Aplenty

Matching uppercase and lowercase letters (RF.K.1d)
Youngsters wiggle into letter knowledge practice with this versatile idea. Label a supply of apple cutouts (patterns on page 65) with different uppercase letters. Then, for each apple, label a worm cutout (patterns on page 65) with the matching lowercase letter. Choose one of the options below.

Center activity: Set out the apples and the matching worms. A child names the letters on each apple. Then she places each worm on its matching apple.

Group activity: Place a large tree cutout on the floor. Put a few apples on the tree and place the matching worms near the tree trunk. Invite a child to take a worm and name the letter. Then lead youngsters in the chant shown as the child picks the matching apple from the tree.

Beth Kickert, T. C. Cherry Elementary, Bowling Green, KY

"A-peel-ing" Apples

Have youngsters make these apples to give their fine-motor skills a workout.

Materials for one apple:
red construction paper apple cutout,
   programmed as shown
white construction paper apple cutout
brown and green construction paper scraps
glue
scissors
stapler

Steps:
1. On the white apple cutout, draw a picture of your favorite food made with apples.
2. Cut along the lines of the red apple.
3. Staple the red apple atop the white apple.
4. Cut a stem from the brown paper scraps and a leaf from the green paper scraps. Write your name on the leaf. Glue the cutouts to the apple.

Diane L. Tondreau-Flohr-Henderson
Kent City Elementary
Kent City, MI

"A-peel-ing" Behavior

Tip

Here's a fresh approach to encouraging positive behavior! Trace a large apple cutout on a paper-backed bulletin board. Then draw a leaf and stem. Next, visually divide the back of the cutout into several sections and number them sequentially. Then cut apart the sections. Whenever students exhibit exceptionally good behavior, post an apple section on the board so the pieces are displayed in order. After the entire apple is assembled, reward the students as desired.

Heather E. Graley, Grace Christian School, Blacklick, OH

Fall Domino Fun

For this small-group game, choose an option below and make game cards as described. To begin a round, one player deals three cards to each player. She stacks the remaining cards facedown and sets the top card faceup on the playing surface. To take a turn, a player places a card beside a card in play so the adjacent domino sections match. For example, she may match the type of objects, the numbers, a number and a set of objects, or a number and a number word. If she does not have a matching card, she takes the top card from the stack. If she does not get a matching card, the next player takes a turn. Players take turns until they cannot play any more cards and no cards are left in the stack.

J. J. Markle, Hanover, PA

Numbers (K.CC.B.5): Color and cut out two copies of the cards from page 66.
Number words (RF.K.3c): Color and cut out two copies of the cards from page 67.
Numbers and number words: Color and cut out one copy each of the cards from pages 66 and 67.

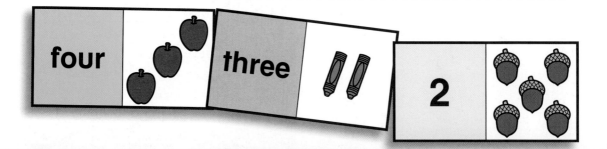

Name_____ Fall

Initial consonants: b, m, r, s (RF.K.3a)

Just Picked!

Cut.

Glue to match the beginning sounds.

The Busy Teacher's Seasonal Book • ©The Mailbox® Books • TEC61439

The Pick of the Crop

 Count the on each .

Write each number.

Color the 🌳 with **more**.

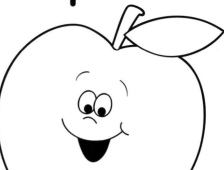

TEC61439

TEC61439

TEC61439

TEC61439

Domino Cards

Use with "Fall Domino Fun" on page 62.

(4 crayons) TEC61439	**1**	(5 acorns) TEC61439	(3 apples)
(5 pencils) TEC61439	**2**	**5**	**5** TEC61439
(2 apples) TEC61439	**3**	**3** TEC61439	(1 crayon)
(3 acorns) TEC61439	**4**	**2**	(5 acorns) TEC61439
(1 bus) TEC61439	**5**	**1** TEC61439	(2 buses)

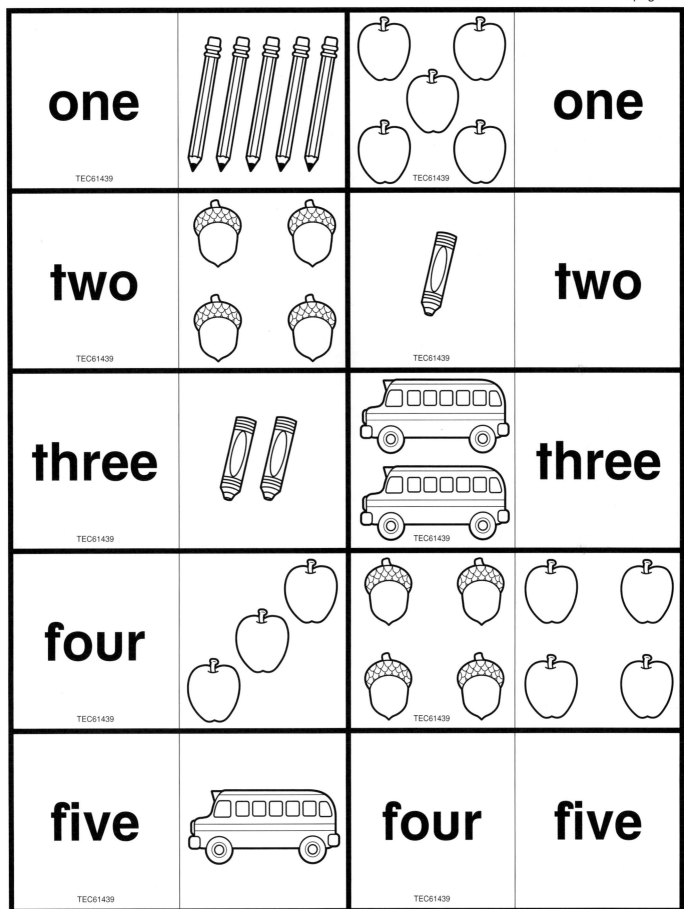

one

one

TEC61439

TEC61439

two

two

TEC61439

TEC61439

three

three

TEC61439

TEC61439

four

TEC61439

TEC61439

five

four   five

TEC61439

TEC61439

Speedy Fire Truck

This project is a perfect token of appreciation for your local firefighters!

Materials for one truck:
4½" x 10" red construction paper rectangle with a slit in one
   long side as shown
white and black construction paper scraps
length of yarn
scissors
glue

Steps:
1. Cut a window and two wheels from black paper. Glue them in place.
2. Cut two long strips and several short strips from white paper. Glue them on the truck to make a ladder.
3. Squeeze some glue on the truck where you want the hose to be. Then arrange the yarn to make the hose.

Hide and Peek

Decomposing numbers (K.OA.A.3)

Promote number sense with a stash of hidden acorns! To begin, pair students. Give each twosome a large disposable cup and five brown cubes or paper squares (acorns). Partner 1 places the acorns on a work surface. Next, Partner 2 covers her eyes as Partner 1 conceals a chosen number of the acorns by placing the cup upside down over them.

Then Partner 2 uncovers her eyes, counts the visible acorns, and tells how many acorns she thinks are hidden. Partner 1 lifts the cup to check. For another round of play, the partners trade roles. **For more advanced students,** give youngsters more acorns.

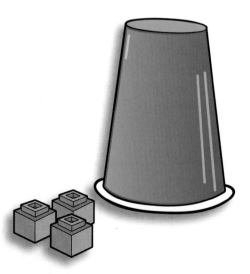

In the
Pumpkin Patch
Syllables (RF.K.2b)

Counting syllables helps this pumpkin patch grow! To prepare for this center, program a large sheet of green paper (pumpkin patch) as shown. Place the pumpkin patch at a center along with a cut-out copy of the cards from page 75. For each card, a child names the picture, quietly claps once for each syllable, and then places the card in the matching row.

Kathryn Davenport
Partin Elementary School
Oviedo, FL

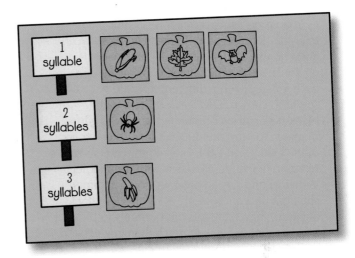

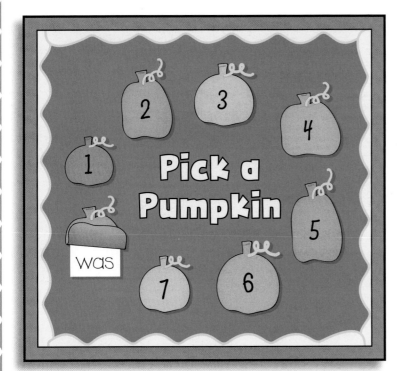

For this fun word review, frame a board or wall space with bulletin board trim. Post the title shown and arrange eight word cards around it. Number eight pumpkins from 1 to 8 and add curling ribbon to resemble vines. Then conceal each card with a pumpkin, securing the pumpkin only at the top. Have youngsters spin a spinner like the one shown. After each spin, lift the corresponding pumpkin and ask students to read the word revealed.
Reading words (RF.K.3c)

Elaina Hall
Mapleton Elementary
Mt. Sterling, KY

Eight Legs

Letter recognition (RF.K.1d)

Youngsters practice letter recognition with this small-group game. To prepare, have each child draw a spider face on a black paper circle. Then have her attach eight sticky dots, each labeled with a different letter, to her spider as shown. Give each student eight black paper strips (spider legs) to use as game markers. To play, announce a letter (keep track of the letters you call). Each child who has that letter on her spider covers it with a spider leg. When a child has all eight legs on her spider, she announces, "Spider!" After checking for accuracy, have students trade spiders to play another round. **For a more challenging version,** announce sounds rather than letters.

Susan Servin, Oracle Ridge School, Oracle, AZ

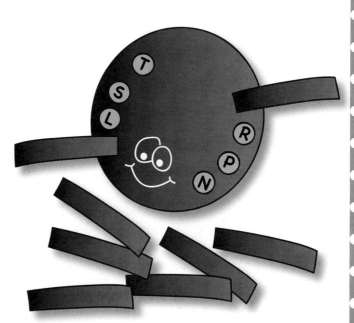

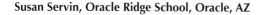

Spiffy Spiders

Each verse of this fun-to-sing song teaches students a spider fact. Introduce the song one verse at a time and challenge students to find the spider fact.

Deborah Davenport-Gibbone
Saint Andrew School
Drexel Hill, PA

(sung to the tune of "The Farmer in the Dell")

I wish I were a spider.
I think it would be fun.
I could use my eight long legs
To help me when I run.

I wish I were a spider.
I'd hang out in a tree.
I could use my many eyes
To see all I could see.

I wish I were a spider.
I think it would be neat.
I could weave a sticky web
And catch a bite to eat.

I wish I were a spider.
I'd dangle from a thread.
I could swing back and forth
And drop on someone's head! Eek!

Go Away, Big Green Monster!

By Ed Emberley

Here's a monstrously fun approach to describing words! Read the book to students. Then instruct each child to use a green circle and provided arts-and-crafts supplies to make a monster head on a black sheet of paper. After each child finishes her artwork, revisit the book and draw students' attention to the describing words. Then invite each child to show her monster to the group and use describing words to tell about it. **For more advanced students,** have each youngster write a brief description of her monster. *Describing words*

Jill Tittsworth, Chief Joseph Elementary, Meridian, ID

My monster has big orange eyes. It has blue hair. It looks funny.
Natasha

Peekaboo Mask

Repeat this idea whenever you need a cute prop for a seasonal song or rhyme.

Materials for one mask:

construction paper scraps	masking tape
large paper plate with precut slit (for viewing)	crayons
	scissors
assorted craft supplies	glue
jumbo craft stick	

Steps:
1. Choose a seasonal object, such as a pumpkin, cat, squirrel, or owl. Then color the paper plate accordingly.
2. Decorate the plate so it resembles the object you chose.
3. Tape the craft stick (handle) to the back of the plate.

Amy Rodriguez
Public School 212
Brooklyn, NY

Fall Fun!

throw

ball

leaves

hide

basket

run

seek

swing

tree

rake

Note to the teacher: Give each youngster a copy of this page. Familiarize students with the words and pictures; then ask each child to keep the paper in her journal or writing folder for easy reference.

Name _____

That's Nutty!

Count. Write.

Color the 🌰 that has **more**.

It's Fall!

Name each picture.

 Color one face for each syllable.

TEC61439

TEC61439

TEC61439

TEC61439

TEC61439

TEC61439

TEC61439

TEC61439

TEC61439

TEC61439

TEC61439

TEC61439

NOVEMBER

To make this Veterans Day display, ask each student to color a copy of a United States flag. Invite her to write holiday-related words or sentences on the white stripes. Curl lengths of red, white, and blue curling ribbon and attach them to each flag as shown. Post students' completed flags on a titled board and then embellish the display with stars.

Linda Teagarden, Dennett Road Elementary, Oakland, MD

Naomi

Cook the turkey for 14 minutes at 600 degrees. Then you can go do your nails and wait for it to cook.

One-of-a-Kind Recipes

Making a class book

Looking for that perfect Thanksgiving gift for parents? Ask each child how she would prepare the Thanksgiving turkey and trimmings and record her response. Then type and print each recipe and have the child illustrate her Thanksgiving meal. Copy the pages and bind the recipes into books for children to give their parents for Thanksgiving.

Laura Petro
Mountview Road School
Morris Plains, NJ

Thankful Pie

Expressing thankfulness

Follow up a discussion on what it means to be thankful with this sweet project. To begin, have each child write, dictate, or draw something she is thankful for on each of several paper strips. Then direct her to fold her strips and put them in an individual-size disposable tart pan. Next, have her paint a tagboard circle (sized to fit inside the rim of the tart pan) with a mixture of equal parts of orange paint and nonmentholated shaving cream plus a dash of pumpkin pie spice. When her circle is dry, have her glue a small piece of cotton batting (whipped cream) to the center and then place it atop the tart pan to make a pumpkin pie. Invite children to take their pies home and share their thankful thoughts with their families on Thanksgiving Day.

Alice McDaniel, Apex, NC

I am thankful for my Mommy.

Find the Feathers!

Reading color words (RF.K.3c)

To prepare this small-group game, cut out a copy of the spinner pattern on page 81. Then attach a paper clip to it with a brad. For each player, glue a turkey head to a small paper plate and make one feather of each of the eight basic colors. (See the patterns on page 81.) Put the feathers in the center of the group.

To take a turn, a player spins the spinner and reads the word on which it lands. If his turkey does not have a feather of the corresponding color, he tucks the end of a matching feather under his plate. If his turkey already has a matching feather, he does nothing. The players take turns as described for the allotted time or until one player's turkey has eight feathers. Then the players compare how many feathers their turkeys have. **For an easier version,** color each section of the spinner the corresponding color.

Andrea Singleton
Waynesville Elementary
Waynesville, OH

Hide and Hunt

To prepare for this small-group game, cut out the pilgrim hat and turkey from a copy of page 82 for each student. Then program the patterns as described in one of the options below. Hide the turkeys around the classroom while students are out of the room. To complete the activity, give each child in the group a hat and encourage him to hunt for the corresponding turkey. After checking each child's match, direct youngsters to swap hats to prepare for another hunt.

Matching numbers: Program each hat with a different numeral and each turkey with an identical numeral.
Matching numbers to sets (K.CC.A.3): Program each hat with a different numeral. For each number, draw a matching dot set on a turkey.
Number words (RF.K.3c): Program each hat with a different numeral. Then write each matching number word on a different turkey.

adapted from an idea by Laurie Gibbons, Huntsville, AL

A Thankful Turkey

Encourage students to take these completed projects home and ask their family members to write on paper strips reasons why they are thankful. Have youngsters place the strips in the bags and then tuck the turkeys away for next year.

Materials for one turkey:
copy of the patterns on page 83
lunch-size brown paper bag
crayons
scissors
glue

Steps:
1. Color and cut out the patterns.
2. Place the bag on the work surface with the flap side down.
3. Glue the feathers to the bag and then glue the turkey head atop the feathers.
4. Open the bag so it stands up; then fold the top of the bag down.

Donna Follett, Kids Inn, Amherst, NH

A Terrific Turkey

These projects are so cute you'll want to show them off! Display them with the title "Our Gorgeous Gobblers!"

Materials for one turkey:
4 pieces of double-sided foam tape
construction paper circles: 8½" brown, 6½" red, 5" orange, 4" yellow, 3" brown
2" x 5" construction paper strips in assorted colors (feathers and legs)
construction paper scraps
scissors
glue

Steps:
1. Use the tape to join the circles from smallest to largest as shown.
2. Trim several paper strips to make feathers and legs; then glue them in place.
3. Cut a beak, a wattle, and two eyes from the paper scraps and glue them in place.

Rosemary Cliburn, Christian Home and Bible School, Mount Dora, FL

A Feast of Good Work

These cute gobblers show off student work samples. Have each youngster illustrate a brown circle and glue it to a scalloped shape to resemble a turkey as shown. Then write each student's name on his turkey's feathers. Post a title and each student's turkey along with a sample of his best work.

80

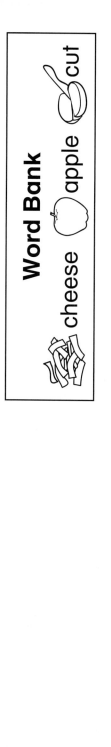

Cut.

Glue in order.

Write.

Dinner for Two

Word Bank

cheese   apple   cut

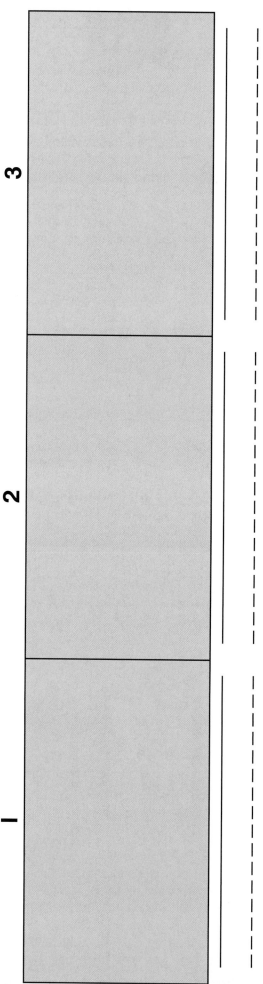

| 1 | 2 | 3 |

Spinner, Turkey, and Feather Patterns
Use with "Find the Feathers!" on page 77.

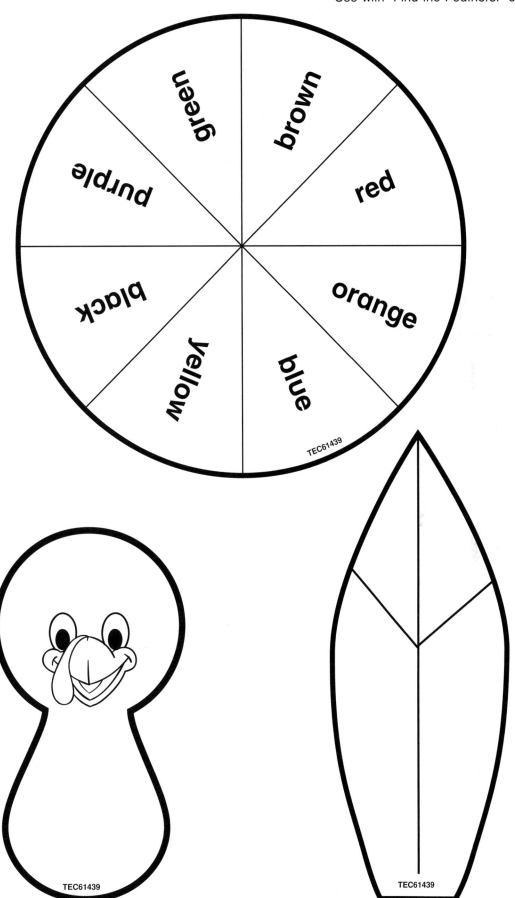

green

brown

purple

red

black

orange

yellow

blue

TEC61439

TEC61439

TEC61439

The Busy Teacher's Seasonal Book • ©The Mailbox® Books • TEC61439

81

Pilgrim Hat and Turkey Patterns
Use with "Hide and Hunt" on page 78.

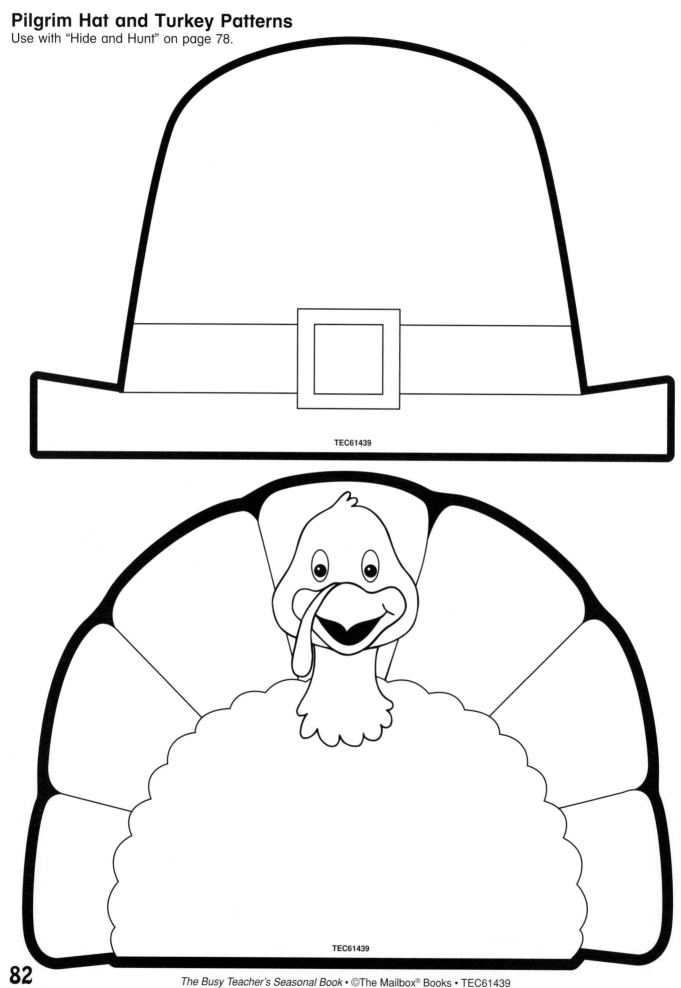

TEC61439

TEC61439

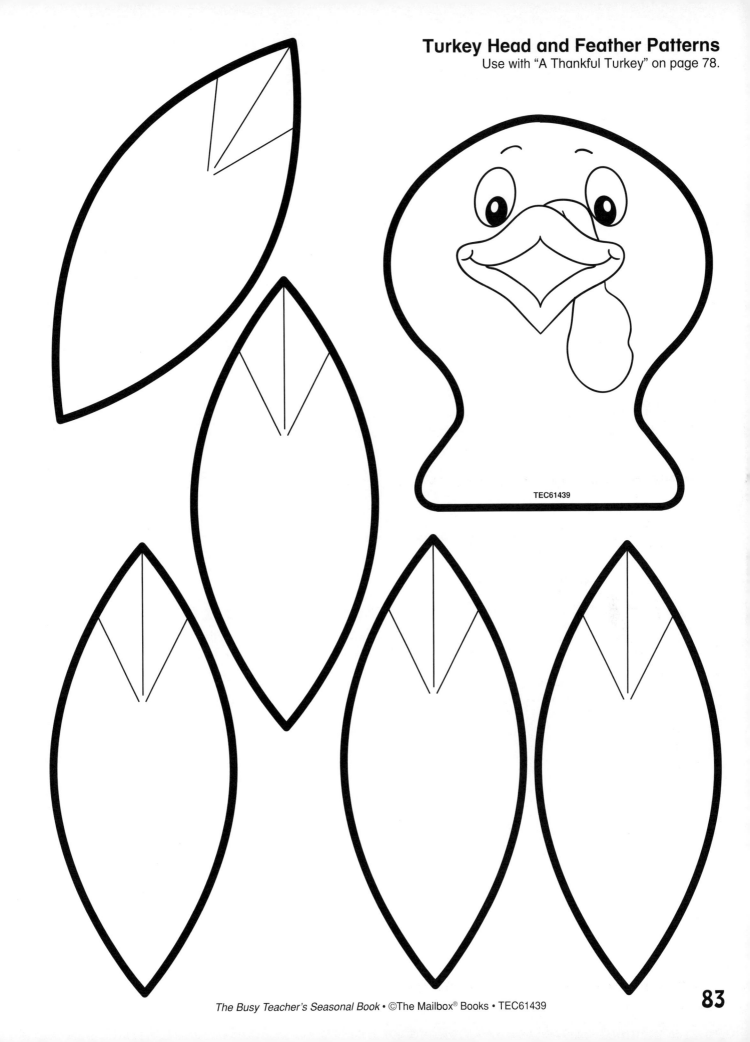

TEC61439

Holiday Candles

Recognizing holidays around the world

Explain to students that many different cultures use candles to represent holiday traditions. Then have each child draw a large candle on the front of a folded sheet of paper and glue on a paper flame. Next, read aloud the poem shown and give each child a copy of the poem to glue inside her paper. Then invite her to take the poem home to share with her family.

Dede Boudinet, Old Bonhomme School, Olivette, MO

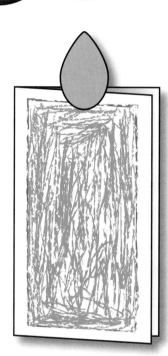

> See the candles shine so bright,
> Burning, blazing day and night.
> On a menorah or on a tree
> Or on a kinara for all to see.
> See the candles shine so bright,
> Welcoming the holidays with their light!

Light the Tree

Add a twinkle to assessments with this easy-to-adapt activity. Program the bulbs on a copy page 91 as described in one of the options below. Working with one student at a time, assess the skill as described. Then highlight the bulb for each correct answer to "light" the tree.

Initial consonants (RF.K.3a): Program each bulb with a different letter. Name a word and have a child point to the beginning letter.
High-frequency words (RF.K.3c): Write a different word on each bulb. Ask a child to read each word.
Number identification (K.CC.A.3): Program each bulb with a different number and have a child name each number.

adapted from an idea by Ilene Bickel
Naples Park Elementary
Naples, FL

Stocking Stuffers

Distinguishing between needs and wants

Display within students' reach two large paper stocking cutouts. Label one stocking "Needs" and the other "Wants." Invite youngsters to cut from magazines pictures of items that are needs or wants. Then gather the class near the stockings and ask each youngster, in turn, to glue his pictures to the correct stockings.

Karen Gore, Dames Ferry Elementary, Gray, GA

Oh, Christmas Tree!

Materials for one tree ornament:
six 1" rings cut from a cardboard tube
construction paper scraps
mini pom-poms
ribbon
green paint
paintbrush
scissors
glue

Steps:
1. Paint the inside and outside of the rings green.
2. When the paint is dry, glue the rings together to make a tree.
3. Glue pom-poms (ornaments) and other desired details to the tree.
4. Tie a length of ribbon to the tree for a hanger.

Suzanne Ward
Caledonia Centennial Public School
Caledonia, Ontario, Canada

Big-Bellied Santa

Hang these jolly fellows on a bulletin board for a "ho-ho-holiday" display.

Materials for one Santa:

copy of page 92
red disposable plastic bowl
cotton balls
crayons

scissors
stapler
glue

Steps:

1. Color and cut out the patterns.
2. Place the bowl upside down and staple the patterns to the rim of the bowl as shown.
3. Stretch out a few cotton balls and glue them to the hat, face, mittens, and boots as shown.

Janice Shuman
Saint Brigid School
South Boston, MA

A Handy Reindeer

Materials for one reindeer:

9" x 12" tan construction paper
white paper plate
red pom-pom
sticky dots
brown paint
paintbrush
scissors
glue
markers

Steps:

1. Paint the plate brown and allow it to dry.
2. Trace both your hands on the tan paper.
3. Cut out the tracings and glue them to the plate so they look like antlers.
4. Add sticky-dot eyes and a pom-pom nose.
5. Draw a mouth.

Amy Rodriguez
Public School 212
Brooklyn, NY

Happy Holidays!

To create this festive tree, have each child make green fingerprints (leaves) on a paper plate. After the paint is dry, invite her to make several red thumbprints (berries) atop the leaves. Then help her attach a trimmed photograph of herself and a red paper bow to her plate to complete her wreath. Post the wreaths above a brown paper rectangle (trunk) to form a tree shape.

Stacy Wingen
Howard Elementary
Howard, SD

Editor's Tip:
Just before the holiday break, have students take the wreaths home to give as gifts.

Kwanzaa Kindness

Working toward a class goal

Promote thoughtful behavior this Kwanzaa season. After explaining the seven principles of Kwanzaa (see chart), draw a large kinara on the board or on chart paper. Explain to students that when the class exhibits one of the seven principles, you will color in one candle on the kinara. After all the candles are colored, reward youngsters with a Kwanzaa-related reward, such as a feast of fruits and vegetables or a party to make mkekas (woven mats).

Gerri Primak
Charlotte, NC

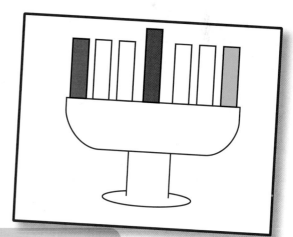

Seven Kwanzaa Principles
Umoja—unity
Kujichagulia—self-determination
Ujima—collective work and responsibility
Ujamaa—cooperative economics
Nia—purpose
Kuumba—creativity
Imani—faith

Name

M Is for Menorah

✏ Write each beginning letter.

✂ 🖌 Cut. Glue the words that start with m.

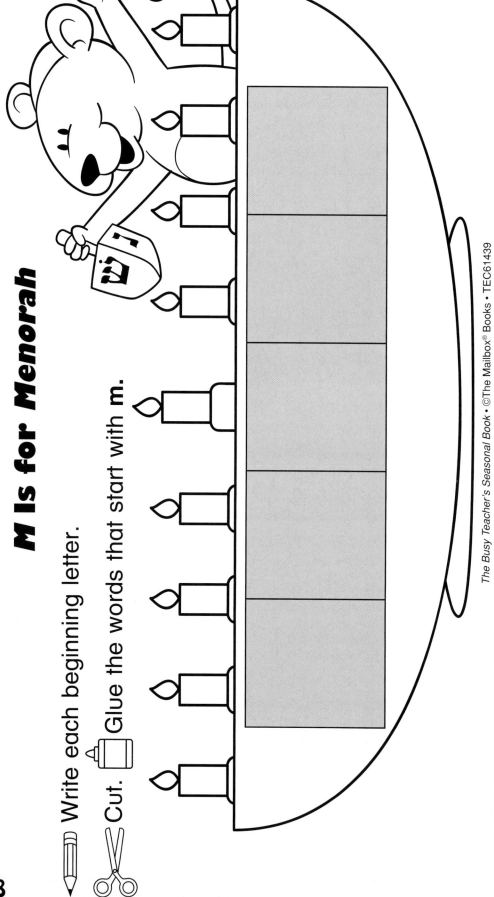

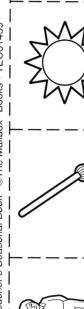

_____ oon

_____ ug

_____ un

_____ op

_____ an

_____ at

_____ ap

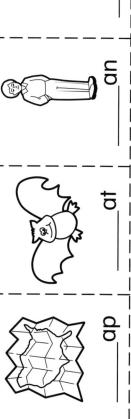

The Busy Teacher's Seasonal Book • ©The Mailbox® Books • TEC61439

Note to the teacher: Have each child follow the directions on the page. Then have him glue the remaining two cards to the back of his paper.

Holiday Words

candle

candy cane

card

gingerbread house

jingle bell

present

tree

wreath

stocking

A Basic Principle

Read.

 A family can work together to wash the dog.

 A family can work together to clean their home.

A family can work together to pick up trash.

 Write. **Draw.**

I can work with my family to _____

_____ .

Light the Tree

The Busy Teacher's Seasonal Book • ©The Mailbox® Books • TEC61439

Note to the teacher: Use with "Light the Tree" on page 84.

91

Santa Patterns

Use with "Big-Bellied Santa" on page 86.

TEC61439

I drink hot chocolate in the winter.

Winter Is...
Writing (W.K.3)
Here's a cool idea that encourages students to write captions. Ask each child to bring to school a winter-related item, such as mittens, a plastic mug for hot chocolate, a scarf, or a paper snowflake. Take a photo of each child holding her item. Have her glue the photo to a sheet of paper. Then direct her to use the word wall and other environmental print to write a caption telling how her item relates to winter. Display the projects with the title "Winter Is Wonderful!"

Betty Silkunas, Lower Gwynedd Elementary, Ambler, PA

A Brand-New Year
Writing (L.K.1f)
Kick off the new calendar year with this class writing activity. To begin, ask students to help compile a class list of things they have learned since the beginning of the school year. Then make another list of things they would like to learn during the remainder of the school year. Display the lists with the poem shown.

Jodi Darter, Cabool Elementary, Cabool, MO

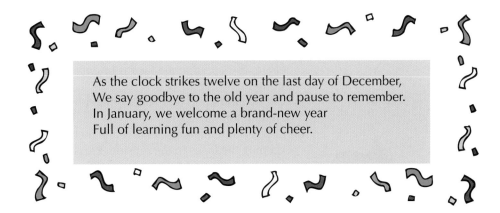

As the clock strikes twelve on the last day of December,
We say goodbye to the old year and pause to remember.
In January, we welcome a brand-new year
Full of learning fun and plenty of cheer.

14

Bring On the Buttons!

Math Center

Build counting or addition skills with a frosty friend! Make a paper snowman with a face and a top hat. Program several sticky notes for an option described below. Place the sticky notes, the snowman, and a supply of small craft foam or tagboard circles (buttons) at a center. Have students complete the activity as described.

Counting (K.CC.B.5): Write a different number on each sticky note. A student attaches a sticky note to the snowman's hat and then places the matching number of buttons on the snowman.

Solving word problems (K.OA.A.2): Write a different addition word problem on each sticky note. A student attaches a sticky note to the snowman's hat and places the corresponding number of buttons on the snowman to solve the problem.

Kristi Miller, Woodward-Granger Elementary, Granger, IA

Dancing Snowpal

Welcome winter with this cool mobile!

Materials for one snowpal:
2 white circles of each of these sizes: 4", 5", 7"
various colors of paper scraps, including orange, brown, and black
scissors
glue
black marker
tape
24" length of string

Steps:
1. Cut out two triangles (noses) from orange construction paper. Glue each triangle on a four-inch white circle. Add marker details to complete each face.
2. Place a seven-inch circle on a work surface and tape one end of the string to it.
3. Position a five-inch circle above the taped circle. Then tape the string to it as shown.
4. Place a four-inch circle facedown above the five-inch taped circle. (Be sure that the face is oriented correctly.) Tape the string to the circle.
5. Cut two arms and two boots from construction paper. Glue them to the snowpal.
6. Glue each remaining circle to the matching taped circle, keeping the faces to the outside. Press the edges of the circles together.
7. Decorate both middle circles as desired.
8. Tie the free end of the string to make a hanger.

Johanna Litts, North Central Elementary, Hermansville, MI

Spark creative thinking with this imaginative display. Have each student use chosen arts-and-crafts materials to make a snowpal. Then ask him to write on a speech bubble a sentence that his frosty friend might say (or dictate the sentence for you to write). Showcase each youngster's snowpal with his sentence on a titled board.

Stephanie Schmidt, Lester B. Pearson Public School, Waterloo, Ontario, Canada

Roly-Poly Penguin

Mount these critters on a snowy background for an adorable winter display.

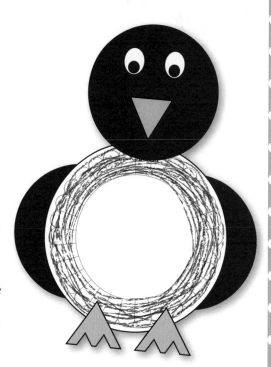

Materials for one penguin:
9" paper plate
two 3" black paper circles
3 orange paper triangles
construction paper scraps

Steps:
1. To make the body, color the rim of the plate.
2. Cut the construction paper scraps to make eyes. Glue the eyes and an orange triangle (beak) to one of the black circles (head).
3. Glue the head to the body.
4. Cut the other black circle in half to make wings. Glue one wing to each side of the body.
5. Cut notches in each of the remaining orange triangles (feet) and glue them to the body.

Lisa Igou, Silbernagel Elementary, Dickinson, TX

Civil Rights Song

Celebrating Martin Luther King Day

Use this little ditty to explore Martin Luther King Jr.'s life.

(sung to the tune of "The Wheels on the Bus")

Some kids said we can't play with you,
Play with you,
Play with you.
Some kids said we can't play with you.
Martin Luther King.

Continue with these lines:
Martin learned the power of words.
Dr. King wanted to change the world.
Dr. King spoke against unfair laws.
Dr. King led a bus boycott.
Dr. King said, "I have a dream."

adapted from an idea by Barbee Stueve, Wilson Arts Integration Elementary, Oklahoma City, OK

A Peaceful Dove

Honor Martin Luther King Jr. with this double-sided project that gives students practice folding and cutting.

Materials for one dove:

large white paper circle	glue
2 equal-size yellow paper	crayons
triangles (beak)	hole puncher
scissors	yarn

Steps:

1. Fold the circle in half, open it, and cut on the fold line.
2. Cut a few slits in one end of a semicircle (body) to look like tail feathers
3. Glue a beak and draw an eye on each side of the body.
4. Fold the other semicircle in half, open it, and cut on the fold line to make two wings.
5. Make a tab on each wing by folding down one of the straight edges. Glue one tab to each side of the body.
6. Hole-punch the top of the project. Thread a yarn length through the hole and tie its ends to make a hanger.

Amy Rodriguez, Public School 212, Brooklyn, NY

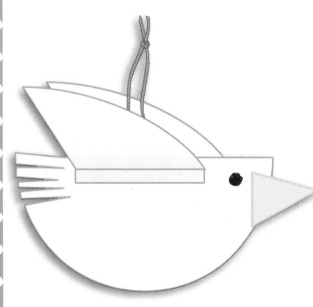

Keeping Warm

 Name each picture.

Count the word parts.

Color a mitten for each word part.

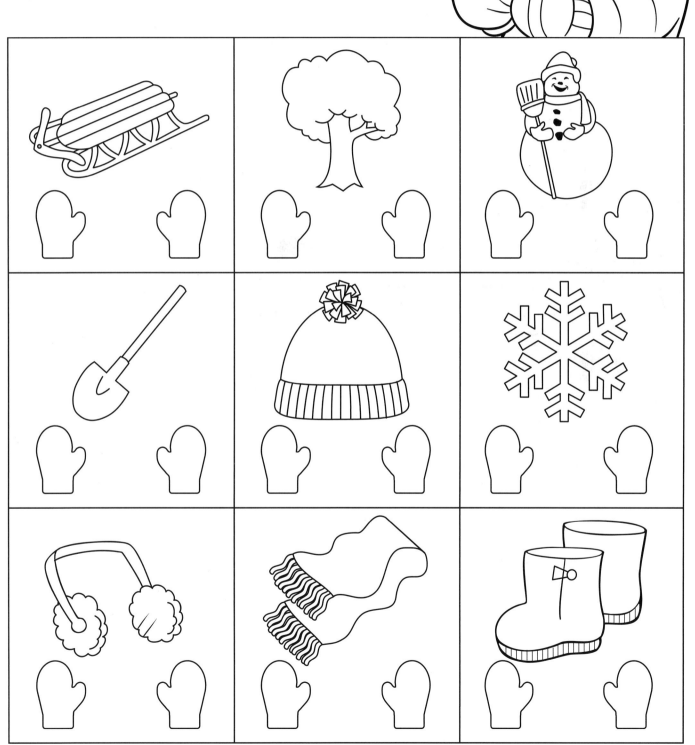

Name _____

Fishing for Snacks

🖍 Color to match the vowel sounds.

ō as in 🦴

ā as in 🐝

Bonus: Which words have the same vowel sound as in 🏵 ? Draw a picture that has those two items in it.

The Busy Teacher's Seasonal Book • ©The Mailbox® Books • TEC61439

Famous Figures

Recognizing Black History Month

Bring Black History Month to life with these kid-size figures. After sharing information about a famous Black American, have a child lie on a length of bulletin board paper; then trace his outline. Cut out the tracing and then help youngsters draw clothes and other details so it resembles the featured person. Attach a nametag to the figure. Then invite volunteers to name facts about the person. Write each fact from the person's perspective on separate paper strips. Display the figure and the facts.

Lois M. Williams
P.S. 209
New York City, NY

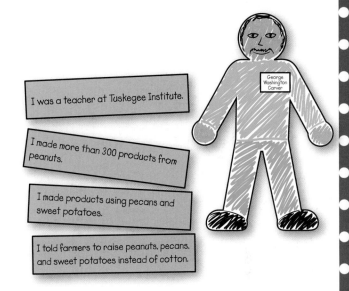

I was a teacher at Tuskegee Institute.

I made more than 300 products from peanuts.

I made products using pecans and sweet potatoes.

I told farmers to raise peanuts, pecans, and sweet potatoes instead of cotton.

George Washington Carver

Terrific for Teeth

Writing (W.K.2)

For National Children's Dental Health Month, make a toothbrush booklet for each student. To make one, fold a long strip of paper in half lengthwise. Staple two white covers and several pages between the paper as shown. Ask each youngster to write her name on her booklet handle and carefully cut the front cover so it looks like bristles. Then have her complete the pages with sentences and illustrations that promote good dental hygiene.

Sara Wendahl, St. Mary's Elementary, Waukesha, WI

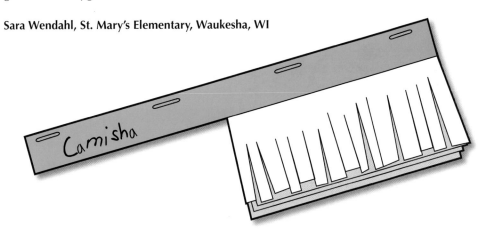

Camisha

Punxsutawney Phyllis

Written by Susanna Leonard Hill
Illustrated by Jeffrey Ebbeler

Phyllis is not a typical groundhog. While other groundhogs huddle in their burrows when the weather is too hot, too cold, or too wet, Phyllis is outside picking blackberries, wading in icy streams, or feeling the mud between her toes. Others laugh at her dream to be the next Punxsutawney Phil. After all, that position is reserved for boys. But on Groundhog Day, Phyllis's keen observation skills prove that she just might be the best groundhog for the job!

After a reading of the story, have youngsters make their own versions of Phyllis popping out of her burrow! Have each child brush glue on a paper cup and then place brown tissue paper over the glue. When the glue is dry, help her cut a slit in the bottom of the cup and insert a simple groundhog stick puppet (pattern below) into the cup. Encourage youngsters to use the puppet to retell parts of the story. **Retelling (RL.K.2)**

Amy Rodriguez, Public School 212, Brooklyn, NY

Groundhog Pattern
Use with *"Punxsutawney Phyllis"* on this page.

TEC61439

Valentine Fun

Literacy or Math Center

Use valentines to review a variety of skills. Set out several boxes of valentines and choose one of the options below.

High-frequency words (RF.K.3c): Write a list of high-frequency words on a heart-shaped chart. Post the chart at a center and set out a supply of paper. A student reads each word; then she looks through the cards to find the words. She keeps a list of each word she finds.

Patterning: A child organizes the cards to make two or more different patterns.

Sorting: A student sorts the cards by a rule of her choice. Then she re-sorts the cards a different way.

Jodi Darter, Cabool Elementary, Cabool, MO

Editor's Tip:
Plan ahead for next year! Purchase cards right after Valentine's Day to get them at a fraction of the cost.

Puppy Love

Made entirely from hearts, this puppy can be used as a valentine or in an eye-catching display.

Materials for one puppy:
2 large hearts (face and ears)
3 small hearts (eyes and nose)
glue
crayons
scissors

Wendy Jumper
Lewisburg Elementary
Olive Branch, MS

Steps:
1. Fold one of the large hearts in half and open it. Cut on the fold line to make two ears.
2. Glue the ears, eyes, and nose to the face, as shown.
3. Use crayons to draw a mouth, pupils, and other desired details.

Heartwarming Card

Deliver a Valentine's Day message with this adorable mouse! To prepare, cut a large heart from a vertical 9" x 12" sheet of tagboard to make a tracer. For each student, cut two three-inch hearts from red paper and two smaller hearts from pink paper.

To make one card, fold a 12" x 18" sheet of red paper in half and then position it with the fold on the left. Trace the tagboard heart, aligning its left side with the fold, and then cut out the tracing. Next, write a holiday message in the card or write the message on a large blank index card and then glue it in the mouse card. To complete the card, draw two eyes above the point of the heart. Glue a pom-pom or a piece of crumpled tissue paper on the point to make a nose. Fold two red hearts and two pink hearts in half and then unfold them. Glue each pink heart on a separate red heart. Then glue the resulting ears in place.

A Ditty About Honest Abe

Recognizing Presidents' Day
Youngsters revisit facts about Abraham Lincoln as you lead them in singing this catchy tune.

(sung to the tune of "When the Saints Go Marching In")

Good Abe Lincoln,
Good Abe Lincoln
Was this land's sixteenth president.
He is known as Honest Abe.
Hip, hip, hooray for Abe Lincoln.

Good Abe Lincoln,
Good Abe Lincoln,
He promised to end slavery.
We see his face on our pennies.
Hip, hip, hooray for Abe Lincoln.

Beth Herchelroath, Oak View Elementary, Fairfax, VA

Name _____

Valentine's Day Deliveries

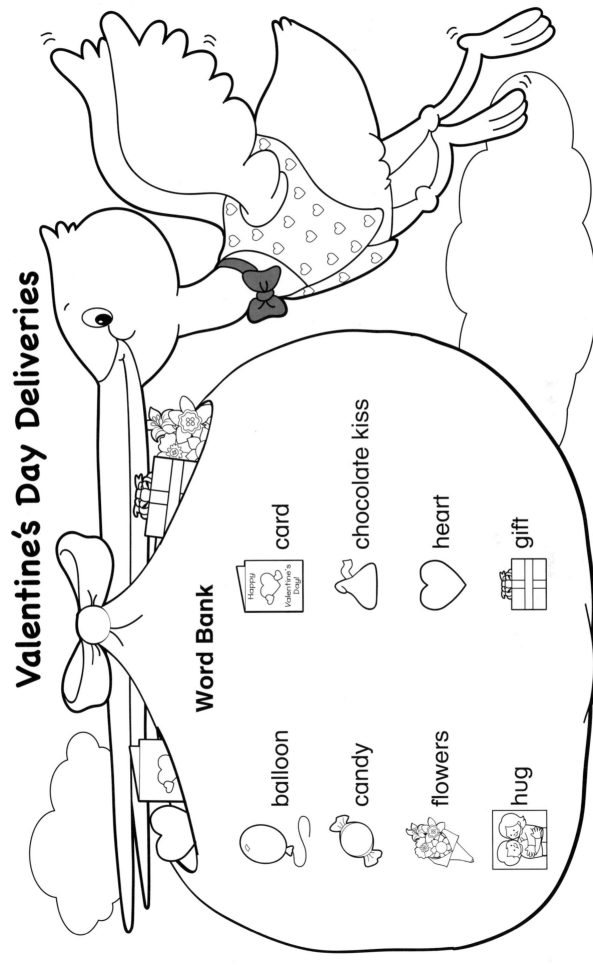

Word Bank

balloon

candy

flowers

hug

card

chocolate kiss

heart

gift

Happy Valentine's Day!

Note to the teacher: Give each child a copy of this page. Read the words aloud and invite him to color the paper as desired. Then ask him to keep the paper in his journal or writing folder for easy reference.

Two Terrific Presidents

Read the [pencil]. Circle two presidents' names.

Cut. Glue.

Presidents' Day is celebrated in February. It is a day to honor George Washington, Abraham Lincoln, and all other presidents.

Bonus: Draw and label a picture of the current president.

The Busy Teacher's Seasonal Book • ©The Mailbox® Books • TEC61439

☆ 16th president	👢 1st president
👢 "Father of His Country"	☆ wanted to stop slavery
☆ Abraham Lincoln	👢 George Washington

MARCH

WELL-BALANCED MEALS

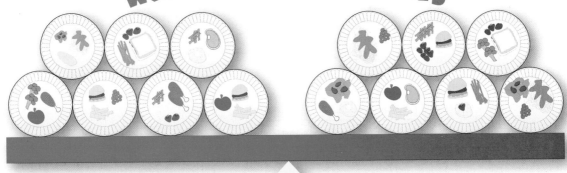

Celebrate National Nutrition Month with this simple display. After students are familiar with the different food groups, have each youngster illustrate a nutritious meal on a white paper plate. Post a jumbo balance scale on the wall. Arrange the student-illustrated plates on the scale and then add a title.

Candice Marshall, Kensington Parkwood Elementary, Bethesda, MD

Read, Read, Read!

Celebrate the anniversary of Dr. Seuss's birthday (March 2) with this catchy song.

(sung to the tune of "Row, Row, Row Your Boat")

Read, read, read a book.
We read all the time.
We all love books by Dr. Seuss.
We love the way they rhyme.

Read, read, read a book.
Read about the cat.
The naughty cat makes such a mess!
What do you think of that?

Read, read, read a book.
We know just the one:
Green Eggs and Ham
   with Sam-I-Am.
Reading is such fun!

Doreen Scheetz, C.A. Dwyer School, Wharton, NJ

Lucky Shamrocks

Initial consonants (RF.K.3a)

To prepare for this partner activity that reinforces initial consonants, cut out a construction paper copy of the shamrock cards on page 109. Program the back of each card with the picture's beginning letter for self-checking. Spread the cards picture-side up on the floor. Also provide a large gold coin or a yellow sponge cut in a coin shape. A child tosses the coin onto a shamrock and names the beginning letter of the pictured item. He checks his answer and then passes the coin to his partner, who takes a turn in the same manner. Students continue as time allows.

Barbara Descavish-Bloom
Resica Elementary
East Stroudsburg, PA

G!

Pots of Gold

Math Center (K.OA.A.1)

For this partner game, prepare a set of cards showing addition problems to ten and another set of cards showing subtraction problems from ten. Also make a copy of a gameboard from page 110 for each child and set out 30 yellow counters (gold). Then choose one of the options below.

To provide addition practice, stack the addition cards facedown. Each child takes an addition card and uses counters to solve the problem on his gameboard's ten frame. The youngster with the larger sum places a counter atop a gold coin on his gameboard. Each child returns his card to the bottom of the stack. Play continues until one student has five coins on his pot.

To provide subtraction practice, stack the subtraction cards facedown. Students play as directed above for addition. The youngster with the smaller difference puts his coin on the pot.

Tannis Rossi
West Brookfield Elementary
West Brookfield, MA

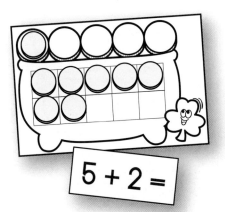

5 + 2 =

1 + 4 =

Pot of Gold

As a follow-up to making this project, have students respond to the writing prompt "If I had a pot of gold…"

Materials for one pot of gold:
copy of the pot pattern from page 111   crayons
puffed corn cereal pieces   scissors
9" x 12" green construction paper   glue

Steps:
1. Color the pot and cut it out.
2. Glue the pot near the bottom of the green paper.
3. Glue the cereal pieces (gold nuggets) above the pot.

Jodi Darter
Cabool Elementary
Cabool, MO

Learning SOARS in Kindergarten

Word Families

Manners and Kindness

Writing: "Lucky the Leprechaun"

Windy Weather

Count to 30

Land and Water

Graphs

Feature students' recent studies with these crafty kites. Instruct each child to decorate a paper diamond (kite) with glitter, paint, or other art materials. Help him tape a length of yarn to his kite. Then have him tie three crepe paper strips to the yarn so they resemble bows. Post the kites with cloud cutouts labeled with topics your students have been learning. As new topics are introduced, post additional cloud cutouts.

Diane Bonica, Deer Creek Elementary, Tigard, OR

High-Flying Friends

Think: What do you like to play with your friends?

Draw.

Where do you play?

What do you play?

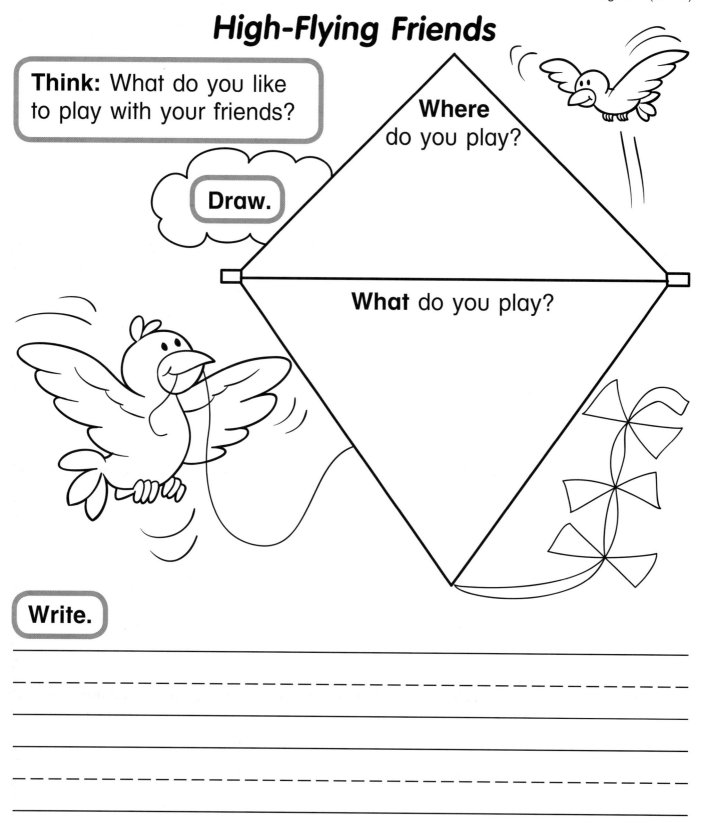

Write.

_____

- -

_____

- -

_____

- -

_____

108

TEC61439

TEC61439

TEC61439

TEC61439

TEC61439

TEC61439

TEC61439

TEC61439

TEC61439

TEC61439

TEC61439

TEC61439

Gameboards

Use with "Pots of Gold" on page 106.

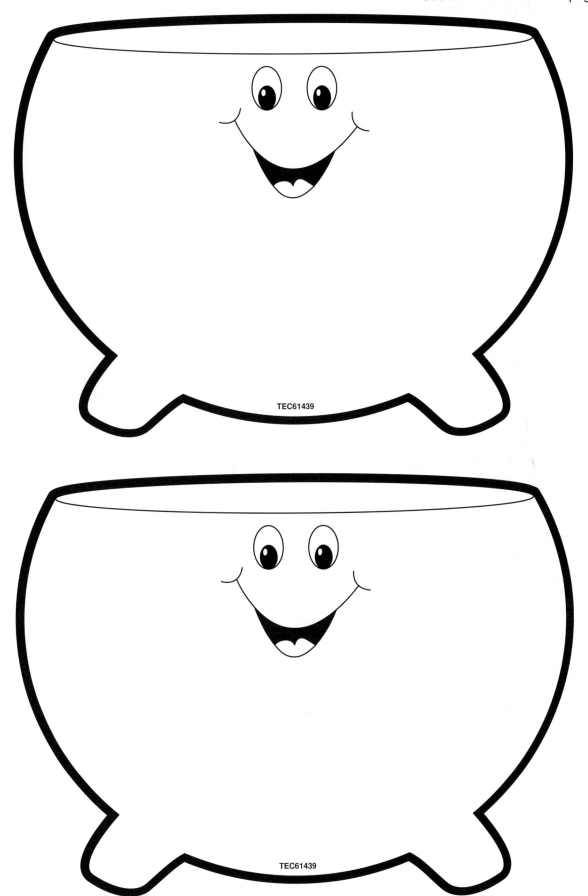

TEC61439

TEC61439

Sweet Bunny

To make this spring scene, fringe-cut one long side of a 4½" x 12" strip of green paper. Glue it to a horizontal 9" x 12" sheet of blue paper, keeping the fringed edge free. Next, trace your shoe on a piece of white paper. Cut out the tracing and draw a bunny face on it as shown. Cut two bunny ears from white paper and color the inner portions pink. Roll the tip of each ear around a pencil. After you glue the ears to the bunny, glue the bunny to the grass and glue a cotton ball to the bunny to resemble a tail.

To complete the scene, fringe-cut one long side of a 2" x 9" strip of green paper. Glue the strip along the bottom of the project, keeping the fringed edge free. Then add details such as torn-paper clouds and flowers made with crumpled pieces of tissue paper.

Sue Lewis Lein, Wauwatosa, WI

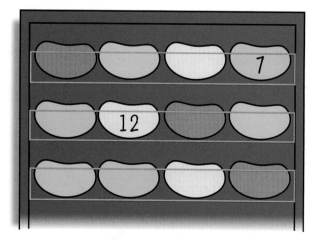

Jumping for Jelly Beans

Counting (K.CC.A.1)

To prepare, write each number from 1 to 20 on a separate jelly bean cutout. Randomly arrange the jelly beans in a pocket chart with the blank sides facing out. Invite a child to turn over a jelly bean and read the number aloud. Then have him lead the group in jumping that number of times. Continue with the remaining jelly beans as time allows.

**adapted from an idea by Rosa Ungurait
Senatobia Elementary
Senatobia, MS**

Twist and Read

Word families (RF.K.3d)

Use plastic eggs to review word families at this seasonal center! Label each right half of several eggs with a different rime. Along the edge of each left half, write beginning letters or blends that make words when combined with the rime. Place the eggs in a basket. A child takes an egg and twists it to read each word. Then he writes the words on a sheet of paper.

Debbie Heide
Lake Linden Hubbell Elementary
Lake Linden, MN

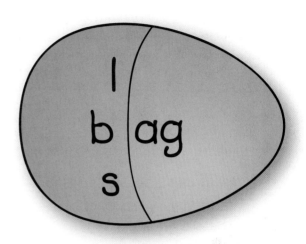

Crack!

High-frequency words (RF.K.3c)

Write high-frequency words on colorful egg cutouts. On another egg cutout, write the word *Crack!* Store the eggs in a bag. To play, invite youngsters, in turn, to pull out an egg and read the word. Play continues until *Crack!* is revealed. Then youngsters count the total number of words read, write the number on a sticky note, and place it on the bag. At a later time, have students play again to try to beat their best score! **For other times of the year,** use different seasonal cutouts and replace *Crack!* with words such as *Boo!* (October); *Gobble, gobble!* (November); *Ho, ho, ho!* (Christmas); and *Drip, drop!* (spring).

Maryann Stewart
Midwestern Intermediate Unit 4
Grove City, PA

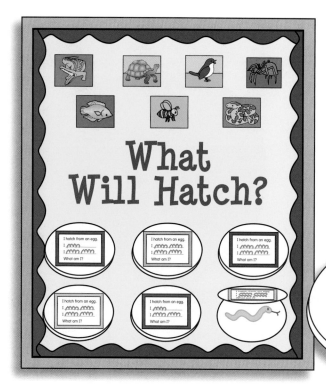

What Will Hatch?

I hatch from an egg.
I
I
What am I?

I hatch from an egg.
I *hiss.*
I *am long.*
What am I?

For this science display, each child completes a riddle like the one below to describe a chosen oviparous animal. He mounts the riddle on colorful paper and glues it to the front of an egg that has been cut from a folded piece of paper. Then he opens the egg and illustrates the animal inside. Display each youngster's egg on a titled board as shown, and post pictures of oviparous animals to jump-start students' guesses.

Tracy Lowe, Des Moines, IA

Grade A Behavior

Tip

Promote positive behavior with this "egg-ceptional" idea! Write a different class reward on each of several small strips of paper. Then fold each strip and place it in a separate plastic egg. Set the eggs in a basket lined with cellophane grass and display the basket in a prominent classroom location. When your class exhibits especially good behavior, invite a child to open an egg and announce the reward to the class.

Patrice Bryson
Hawk Ridge Elementary
Charlotte, NC

extra recess time

Tweet, Tweet!

These baby birds are just in time for spring!

Materials for one nest:

6 cotton balls
7" brown paper circle
3 yellow paper diamonds
black paper scrap

blue marker
glue
hole puncher
scissors

Steps:

1. Cut one-inch slits around the brown circle and fold the edges up to make a nest.
2. Color the cotton balls blue. Glue pairs together (one cotton ball atop the other) in the nest to form the body and head of three birds.
3. Hole-punch six circles in the black paper to make eyes. Glue two eyes to each bird's head.
4. Fold the diamonds in half to make beaks and glue them on to complete the birds.

Sue Fleischmann, Sussex, WI

Good for the Earth!

Learning recycling rules

To prepare for this fun game, gather a class supply of plastic containers that show recycling symbols with various numbers. Have students sit in a circle and then give each child a container. Play a musical recording and direct students to pass the containers around the circle. When the music stops, prompt each child to search for and then identify the number on her container. Have all the youngsters holding containers labeled with the number one stand up. Then tell students that this number is one that most recycling centers will accept. Restart the music and repeat the activity with the number two, explaining this number is also accepted by most recycling centers.

Sarah Hibbett
Henderson, TN

Leaping Lily Pads

Modeling subtraction (K.OA.A.1)

Youngsters pretend to be frogs with this whole-group activity. To prepare, attach green yarn to the floor in the shape of a large lily pad. Invite a desired number of students (frogs) to crouch on the lily pad. Tell a subtraction story, such as "Five frogs are on a lily pad. Three jump off. How many frogs are on the lily pad now?" Then lead a corresponding number of frogs in jumping off the pad to determine the answer. Invite the seated students to explain how the frogs solved the story problem. Continue until each child has a turn to be a frog. **To extend the activity,** write on the board the subtraction problem that matches the story.

Kathy Ginn
Jeffersonville Elementary
Jeffersonville, OH

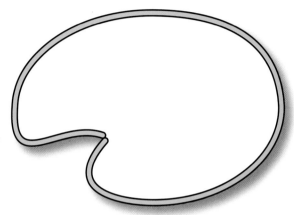

Fantastic Froggies

Craft

Hop into spring with these cute frog planters! For each child, punch a hole near the rim of a green container, such as a plastic drinking cup. Next, help him scoop a mixture of potting soil and grass seeds into the container. Help him tape a large paper eye to each of two green pipe cleaner halves and "plant" the eyes in the soil mixture. Then have the child twist a red pipe cleaner through the hole so it looks like a tongue. If desired, provide paper scraps for him to cut out a fly and glue it to the tongue. Invite each child to keep his frog planter in a sunny place and water it daily. **To extend the activity,** have students keep a daily journal to show the growth of the grass.

Angela Morris
Jefferson Elementary
North Platte, NE

Splish! Splash!

cloud

house

rainbow

flowers

puddle

sun

frog

rain

towel

☐ A rainy day means…   ☐ Mud makes…

☐ When it rains,…   ☐ The sound of rain…   ☐ I wish…

The Busy Teacher's Seasonal Book • ©The Mailbox® Books • TEC61439

Note to the teacher: Have each child keep a copy of this page in his journal-writing folder. After he uses a prompt, ask him to draw a check mark in its box.

Flower Patch

Addition (K.CC.A.1)

How does this garden grow? With addition! Gather a supply of adhesive dots of two different colors. Place the dots, a number cube, white paper, and crayons at a center. To complete the activity, a student rolls the number cube. Then he puts the corresponding number of like-colored dots on his paper, leaving space between them. He rolls the cube again to find out how many dots of the other color to add to his paper. Once his paper has two sets of dots, he incorporates each dot into a flower illustration. Then he labels his work to show how many flowers there are in each set and how many flowers there are in all.

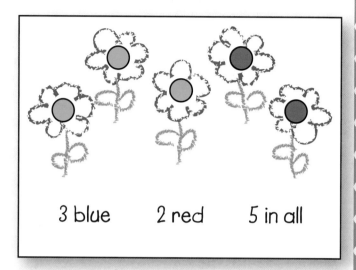

3 blue   2 red   5 in all

A Beautiful Garden

The prints in this project are made using two-liter plastic bottles. Even students with fine-motor delays will find it easy to make a gorgeous garden.

Materials for one garden:
large sheet of construction paper
empty two-liter plastic bottles
shallow containers of paint
pom-poms
green marker
glue

Steps:
1. Use the bottoms of the plastic bottles to make prints on the paper. Allow the paint to dry.
2. Glue a pom-pom to the center of each print so the prints resemble flower blossoms.
3. Draw stems, leaves, and grass.

Heidi Thompson
Lodi, CA

Ladybug Card

Have each student give this card to a loved one as a special Mother's Day gift.

Materials for one card:

copy of a message card from page 123   brad
two 6" red paper circles   scissors
3" black paper circle   glue
black ink pad

Steps:

1. Use the ink pad to make fingerprints (spots) on one of the red circles.
2. When the ink is dry, fold the spotted circle in half. Then unfold it and cut on the crease.
3. Glue the black circle (head) to the other red circle as shown.
4. Sign your name on the message card. Then glue it to the center of the intact red circle.
5. Use the brad to attach the two cut halves (wings) to the intact circle.

Debbie Hill, Stone Elementary, Crossville, TN

Butterfly Buddy

When a student takes home this eye-catching project, she can use it to display her favorite schoolwork on her refrigerator.

Materials for one butterfly:

tagboard copy of a butterfly pattern from page 123
5" square of clear transparency
spring-type clothespin
magnetic tape
permanent markers
scissors

Steps:

1. Trace the butterfly onto the transparency with a permanent marker.
2. Use the markers to color the butterfly.
3. Cut out the butterfly. Then glue it to the clothespin, making sure the closed part is at the bottom.
4. After the glue dries, adhere a strip of magnetic tape to the clothespin as shown.

Cheryl Bowne, Austin Christian Academy, Austin, TX

What's the Buzz?

Reading comprehension (RL.K.2)

Students retell a story with the help of a bumblebee! After a student hears a story or reads a book, give him a copy of page 124. Encourage him to write or draw to complete the graphic organizer. Next, have him cut out the bee pattern. Then help him tape one end of a length of string to the bee and the other end to the back of his paper. Invite each youngster to move the bee to each section of the hive as he tells the story to a partner.

Ana Catasus
Mother of Christ Catholic School
Miami, FL

Name Cooper
Reading comprehension

Title
The Very Hungry Caterpillar

Beginning
It came out of an egg.

Middle
It ate a lot of food.

End
It turned into a butterfly.

Buzzing Along

Program a class supply of yellow hexagon cutouts (honeycomb cells) to match one of the options below. Attach the honeycomb cells to the floor to make a path. Then invite your busy bees to join you for some learning fun.

Letter-sound correspondence (RF.K.3a): Label the honeycomb cells with letters. Invite students to make a buzzing sound as they slowly move along the path. When you say, "Stop!" each youngster stops on a cell. Then have each child, in turn, announce the letter and its sound.

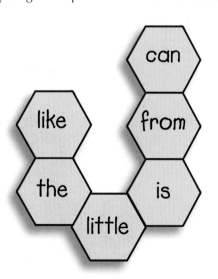

can
like from
the is
little

Number recognition (K.CC.A.3): Label the honeycomb cells with numbers. Have youngsters make a quiet buzzing sound as they move along the path. When you call out a number, the student(s) who is on or closest to the number you called makes a loud buzzing sound.

High-frequency words (RF.K.3c): Label the honeycomb cells with words. Have youngsters quietly read each word as they walk along the path. After a short amount of time, announce one of the words. Each child standing on a cell with that word makes a buzzing sound as he travels to the hive (a predetermined area of the room).

adapted from an idea by Roberta M. Neff
Espy Elementary
Kenton, OH

Mixed-Up Tulips

✏️ Unscramble the letters.
✏️ Write the word.
🖍️ Color the matching 🐞.

have

feel

like

here

you

the

was

see

reeh

eefl

aws

uyo

evah

kiel

het

ese

Bonus: Write the words in **ABC** order.

Name _____

122

All Aflutter

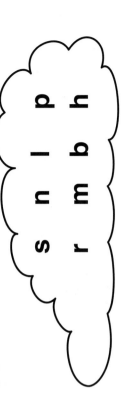

s n l p
r m b h

✏️ Write the beginning letter.

✏️ Cross out the matching letter.

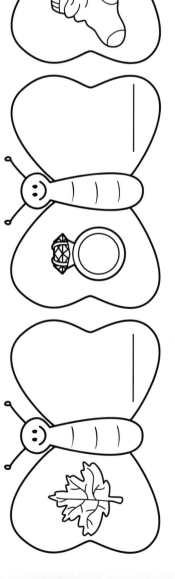

I spotted
the best mom
in the world—
YOU!

TEC61439

I spotted
the best mom
in the world—
YOU!

TEC61439

Butterfly Patterns
Use with "Butterfly Buddy" on page 119.

TEC61439

TEC61439

Name_____ Reading comprehension

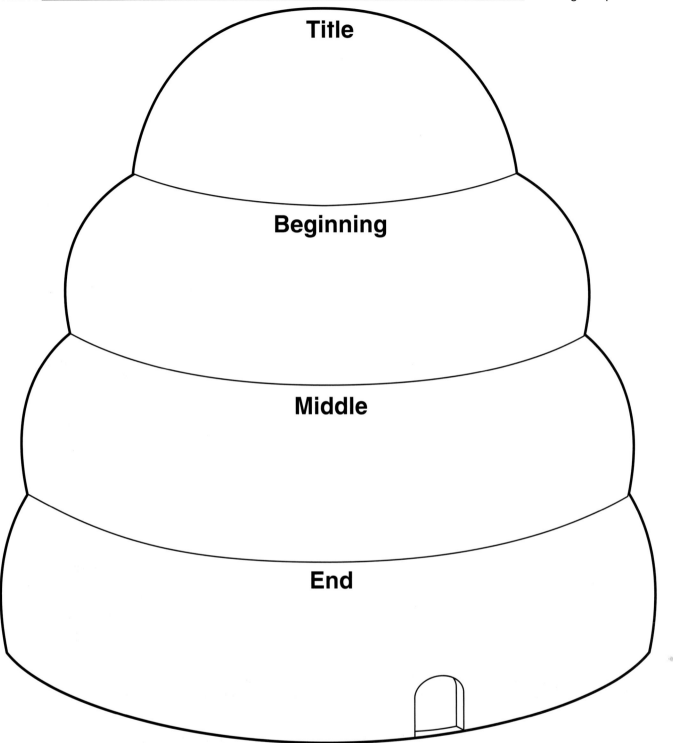

Title

Beginning

Middle

End

Note to the teacher: Use with "What's the Buzz?" on page 120.

Sunny Words

Making words (RF.K.3)

This bright center highlights students' word blending skills. Program a class supply of yellow paper circles (suns) with a rime and write on cards different onsets, most of which form real words when coupled with the rime. Set out the programmed materials, orange paper strips (rays), and writing paper. A child places a card in front of the rime and reads the word. If it is a real word, she writes the word on a ray and glues it to the sun. After adding several rays to the sun, she writes sentences using the words.

Jennifer Reidy, Halifax Elementary, Halifax, MA

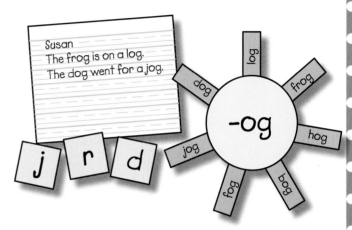

Picnic Fun

Youngsters practice several skills with this easy-to-adapt idea. Program cards as described in one of the options below and store the cards in a picnic basket. Place a blanket on the floor and set the basket nearby. Invite a group of youngsters to join you on the blanket and complete the chosen activity.

Color words (RF.K.3c): Program each of several cards with a different color word. A child takes a card and names an item of that color that she might see at a picnic.

Initial consonants (RF.K.3a): Program each of several cards with a different consonant. A child takes a card and names a picnic food or activity whose name begins with the chosen letter.

Descriptive words: Attach to each of several cards a picture of a picnic food. A child takes a card and uses descriptive words to describe the food.

Marie E. Cecchini
West Dundee, IL

Festive Fireworks

The prints in this project are made by reusing gift bows.

Materials for one project:
9" x 12" black construction paper
gift bows in a variety of shapes and sizes
shallow containers of red, white, and blue paint
silver glitter

Steps:
1. Dip a gift bow in paint. Press the bow onto the paper.
2. Repeat with different bows and colors.
3. While the paint is still wet, sprinkle glitter on the resulting fireworks.
4. After the paint dries, gently shake off the excess glitter.

Sue Fleischmann; Mary, Queen of Saints School; West Allis, WI

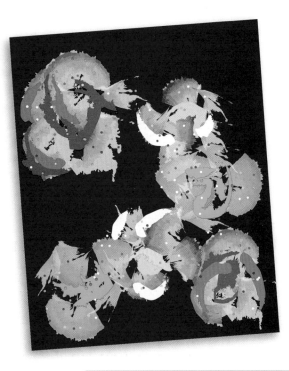

Under the Sea

To wrap up a unit on ocean life, invite each youngster to make an underwater scene.

Materials for one scene:
sand
12" x 18" light blue construction paper
construction paper scraps
ink pads in various colors
glue
diluted glue
paintbrush
markers
scissors

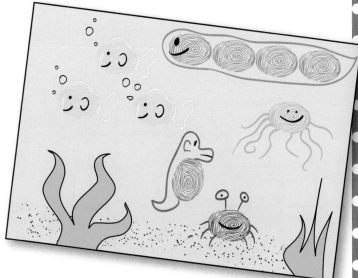

Steps:
1. Make several fingerprints on the paper using different colors of ink.
2. Use the markers to add details to the fingerprints so they look like sea creatures.
3. Cut paper scraps so they resemble seaweed and other plant life. Glue them to the paper.
4. Lightly brush diluted glue on the bottom of the paper. Sprinkle sand on the glue and shake off the excess.

Kelsea Wright, Seal Elementary, Douglass, KS

A Yummy Cookout

 Cut.  Glue in order.

 Write.

1	2	3

_____

- -

_____

- -

_____

- -

_____

- -

_____

- -

_____

Super Sand Castle

Write each beginning and ending letter.

 ___ a ___    ___ i ___

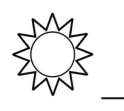 ___ u ___    ___ e ___

 ___ o ___   ___ u ___

 ___ i ___   ___ a ___

 ___ e ___    ___ o ___

128